The Voice of the Apostolic Woman

Apostle Dr. Yvonne Lee-Wilson

www.WeAreAPS.com

ISBN: 978-1-945145-31-5

APS Publishing
312-588-9465
www.WeAreAPS.com

Table of Contents

Dedication

Prologue

Chapter One   The Office of Apostle

Chapter Two   5 *W's* of an Apostle

Chapter Three   Vision Comes to Pass
                       (Habakkuk 2:2)

Chapter Four   Knowing Your Grace as an Apostle

Chapter Five   The Apostolic Woman

Chapter Six   The Male Apostle's Perspective

Chapter Seven   12 Voices of the Apostolic Woman

Chapter Eight   Ministry Begins with Me

Chapter Nine   Purpose for My Pain

Chapter Ten   Reflection of My "Yes!"

Chapter Eleven   Journey of a Servant

Chapter Twelve   The Voice that Bears Truth

12 *Do's & Don'ts* of the Apostolic Woman

Epilogue   Birthing Out

Ministries of Support

The Apostles' Creed:
I believe in God, the Father Almighty,
maker of heaven and earth;

And in Jesus Christ his only Son, our Lord;
who was conceived by the Holy Spirit,
born of the Virgin Mary,
suffered under Pontius Pilate,
was crucified, dead, and buried;*
the third day he rose from the dead;
he ascended into heaven,
and sitteth at the right hand of God the
Father Almighty;
from thence he shall come to judge the
quick and the dead.

I believe in the Holy Spirit,
the holy catholic** church,
the communion of saints,
the forgiveness of sins,
the resurrection of the body,
and the life everlasting. Amen.

DEDICATION

Praise God! This day has finally come, when I truly can release what God gave me over 30 years ago. I never knew I would be in a place like this…or that my pain would become my purpose in life to advance the kingdom of God, for such a time as this.

First, I thank God for being my Savior, Lord, Keeper and Deliverer. It has been 36 years, and I still love Jesus, Son of the Living God. Had it not been for Jesus, I don't know if I would have made it this far. By the grace of God, I am still here to obey and do whatever God has charged me to do.

To my mother, Elder Louise Snipes and my aunt, Rev. Evy Johnson, I love you for pouring into me even when I wasn't ready; you always believed in me. Mother, you taught me how to be strong in the midst of many adversities. Thank you for not allowing the doctors to amputate my right ankle. It is because of God and you; I am standing, walking, shouting and running to obey Him. Thank you for showing me tough love, so I could be a good under shepherd. Thank you for helping me with my **daughters:**

Shantina Lee, Prophet Taneshia Lee, and Tarina Lee (in glory, 2003)

My 8 grandchildren:

Phillip Mardis, Amber Mardis, Jaleel Mardis, Brittany Mardis, Evelene Lee, Brianna Lee, Jene Lee (in glory), and Justin Lee

My 5 great grandchildren:

Kynnedi, Kaelyn, Kamora, Jacoby, and Jakari

You've been an amazing mother-in-law to my husband of 33 years, Adelbert Wilson. To all 8 of my siblings: Carl Lee Jr., Bishop Dr. Anthony Lee, Minister Reginald Lee (in glory), Elder Geneva Davis, Pastor Kenneth Lee, Ray Lee, Brother Travis Lee, and Sister Evelene Lee-Cole, I love all of you. Mother, I praise God! You are my role model and example of an apostolic woman.

To my husband, **Adelbert Wilson**, thank you for speaking into my life everything God told you that I would be...Here I am. More than anything, I serve Him with your support and wisdom. In the midst of all your health challenges, you never held me back. Thank you and I give God the glory for your real love for me.

To my spiritual father, **Dr. Bishop M. Cofield** (in glory) and Evangelist Rose Jones (in glory), you both left me with mantles that I felt unworthy to receive, but I know that God has ordained it for such a time as this. Tests and trials have been too many to count, but I honor the covering that has been released to me to move forward…

Who would have known, but God, that I would be an apostolic woman and would be sharing that it's our finest hour? We are better together than we are apart. Women of God, we need each other. We must empower our men to know it's not about gender but the kingdom and Calvary.

The Lord has graced me to know so many women apostles who have truly blessed and encouraged me in this apostolic walk. The women's names I am about to mention are priceless and I am grateful our paths have crossed in many different ways: Apostle Edith Wright, Apostle Veronica Lopez, Apostle Shanette Hougton, Apostle Gloria Dawson, Apostle Beverly London, Apostle Gloria Hopkins, Apostle Sherain Lathan, Apostle Dr. Barbara Jefferson, Apostle Sharon Peters, Apostle Margie Hardermon, Apostle Frankie Williams, Apostle Deborah Gaines and Apostle Glendora Harris.

Apostle Dr. Carol Sherman is a woman of great faith and purposed to advance the kingdom of God. Apostle Sherman is married to Apostle Duane Sherman who stands as a general to support the work she does across the nation. Apostle Sherman is an author, educator, mother, friend, confidant, worshipper, grandmother, devil buster, intercessor and so much more. We met doing work in the kingdom of God, winning souls on the street during a revival. I received my degree in theology from Ramah Bible Institute. Many challenges have come; sickness and affliction only came to empower her to do more work to win souls for the King. This woman of God truly is an apostle of apostles.

Apostle Beverly London was inspirational in assisting us with establishing the purity sisters for three years. The purity sisters were a group of young ladies who vowed to obey God. Since that time, one has transitioned; Mother Zodie Richardson and the other young ladies are still standing. Some believe God for their mates who God has chosen for them. Woman of God, your integrity and humility precedes everywhere you go. Thank you for interceding for the Body of Christ.

I extend a special tribute to my sister who now lives in Atlanta, Georgia – This woman of God has known me over 40 years and truly she can tell some of my story. It is because of her, I love shoes today. She is truly an apostolic woman. I give God all the glory for the amazing, anointed and appointed, **Apostle Dr. Elsie Bridges**, the trailblazer for women apostles, for such a time as this.

To every chief apostle and apostle, man or woman, these are the last days. Let us come together and do the great commission and compel the loss, the sinner man, and maybe even some saints, what we must do to get saved and maintain our deliverance. This book is to challenge you to accept the call, function in your call, perfect your call and more than anything else, believe you have been called. The apostolic woman is a natural woman with a divine purpose to obey God in every area of her life.

I would also like to acknowledge:

Apostle Charlene Benson

Apostle Lenora Garmin

Apostle Barbara Weathersby

Apostle Veronica Lopez

Apostle Deborah Alexander

Apostle Sheila Anderson

Apostle Gwen Anderson

Apostle Anita Edison

Apostle Maxine Williams

Apostle Gloria Hopkins

Apostle Darlene Young

Apostle Glendora Harris

Chief Apostle Kathleen Miles

Apostle Cheryl Perry Jackson

Thank you so much for all you have done.

FIVE FOLD MINISTRY

The *Evangelist* is represented by the longest finger reaching out to the world, spreading the gospel of Jesus Christ.

The *Prophet* is represented by the pointer (finger). The prophet points towards the way of correction, revealing the Rhema (Word) of God.

The *Pastor* is represented by the ring finger, for the pastor is married to the Church.

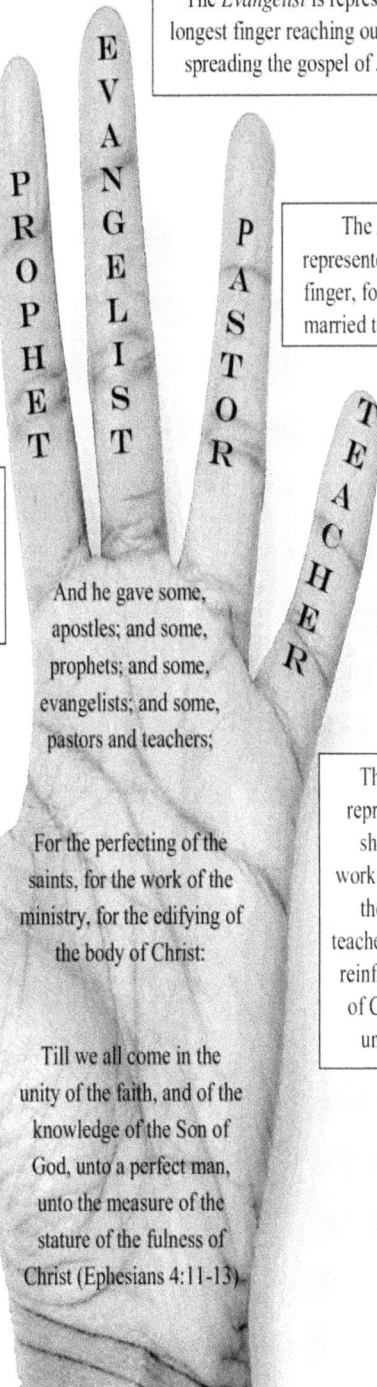

E
V
A
N
G
E
L
I
S
T

P
R
O
P
H
E
T

P
A
S
T
O
R

T
E
A
C
H
E
R

The *Apostle* is represented by the thumb, which is able to touch all other fingers. The Apostle can function in each Office of the Five Fold Ministry.

APOSTLE

And he gave some, apostles; and some, prophets; and some, evangelists; and some, pastors and teachers;

For the perfecting of the saints, for the work of the ministry, for the edifying of the body of Christ:

The *Teacher* is represented by the shortest finger, working closely with the pastor. The teacher highlights and reinforces teachings of Christ for basic understanding.

Till we all come in the unity of the faith, and of the knowledge of the Son of God, unto a perfect man, unto the measure of the stature of the fulness of Christ (Ephesians 4:11-13).

PROLOGUE

This book was inspired by the Holy Ghost, for God's people perish for the lack of knowledge. As Believers, we should live a life that is purposeful for the kingdom of God. Although we have seen evidence in the earth that God does not have respect of persons, it is still challenging for God's people to distinguish between God's plan and personal views.

This writing is centered on facts. God uses whom He will because He is sovereign and almighty. Let's refer to Scripture. *For I know the thoughts that I think towards you, saith the Lord, thoughts of peace and not of evil to give you an expected end (Jeremiah 29:11).* It is an honor and privilege to be called by God. Our God in His infinite wisdom already knew what it would require for His plans in the kingdom to be fulfilled. As we read in the book of Genesis, it was God who created all things using His authority and the power of His spoken word.

If you can accept creation coming into being through the spoken word of God, then why is it so challenging for many to believe the same God spoke the apostolic woman into existence? The office of Apostle has nothing to do with gender and everything to do with God's authority to choose whom He will, for He is sovereign. Many times, we miss the move of God, for we are hindered by the package in which His word is presented. We must be careful not to miss the message, due to issues accepting the messenger. God does not call the qualified; He qualifies the called (Romans 8:28-30).

When we begin to study this scripture more in-depth, it is evident that God's plan did not decipher between sex and gender but was preordained for *the called – those whom He foreknew and predestined to be conformed to the image of His son.*

I am eternally grateful knowing the Lord is faithful and will fulfill His purpose in me! When I reflect upon the trials which I have been forced to endure, it was all in God's plan.

The constant scrutiny, adversity, and persecution mark the journey of the Believer, the disciple, and the apostolic woman, but I must proclaim, according to Philippians 3:13-14, *Brethren, I count not myself to have apprehended: but this one thing I do, forgetting those things which are behind, and reaching forth unto those things which are before, I press toward the mark for the prize of the high calling of God in Christ Jesus.* **Salute Andronicus and Junia, my kinsmen and my fellow prisoners, who are of note among the apostles, who also among the apostles who also were in Christ before me (Romans 16:7).**

How historical is it for Paul who went above and beyond to persecute the early church to be the one to impact destiny by revealing that the apostolic woman existed in his time? If Apostle Paul acknowledged her existence and the fact that she knew what it was to have relationship in Christ Jesus, then why is she still a mystery waiting to be revealed? Why is acceptance in the body of Christ hindered based on her sex? Galatians 3:28 states, *There is neither Jew nor Greek, there is neither bond nor free, there is neither male nor female: for ye are all one in Christ Jesus.*

If salvation is now offered as a choice through the shedding of blood for the remission of sin, then why is God's choice of whom He calls and equips still unaccepted among some Believers? John 15:16 states, *Ye have not chosen me, but I have chosen you, and ordained you, that ye should go and bring forth fruit, and that your fruit should remain; that whatsoever ye shall ask of the Father in my name, he may give it you.*

It cannot be disputed that women have been used to advance the Kingdom. The Bible clearly presents examples of women who were very instrumental to the work of the Lord in the early church. After all, it was a woman who first carried the Gospel and her name was Mary, the mother of Jesus. Queen Esther was anointed to deliver a nation. These women were not anointed by God because of their gender; they were chosen because of the position in which they had been placed in the Kingdom. God strategically designed a position for everyone that will be a part of His kingdom. If you choose to come into alignment with the assignment given, God's purpose shall be fulfilled. God is omniscient, or all knowing. He knew who would be willing, committed and faithful to His plans, despite gender.

CHAPTER ONE:

THE OFFICE OF APOSTLE

In reading the Gospels, we will find that when Jesus began His ministry in the earth, there were twelve men, by divine appointment, who were assigned to walk with Him as His disciples. We also know that later they would be known as the Apostles. Let us define the meaning of *Disciple*. A Disciple is a follower and student of a mentor, teacher, or any wise person. Someone who embraces and is committed to spreading the teachings of another is the essential definition of a disciple. The 12 Disciples who followed Jesus were ordinary men, but their purpose in the kingdom of God made the difference.

I am an ordinary being, but my purpose in the Kingdom commands a lifestyle that must align with the Word of God which will certainly make the difference in my life as well as others who I encounter. Therefore, total transformation is necessary for the mission which I must fulfill. As I reflect upon those who laid the foundation for me to carry the Mantle of Ministry, I am humbled by the life-changing experience, from a new creature in Christ to Chief Apostle.

The Disciples needed teaching and training before they would be able to do the work of the ministry. It was at this time when they witnessed Jesus' interactions with the people and experienced examples of the foundation being laid for the early church. It was not until Jesus had ascended back to heaven that true purpose was revealed. Simply speaking, the student would now become the teacher.

The 12 Disciples were now the 12 Apostles of Jesus. The term, *Apostle,* means *messenger, ambassador or one who is sent to proclaim the gospel.* An apostle is a Christian leader who is gifted, taught, commissioned and sent by God with the authority to establish the foundational government of the church, within an assigned sphere of ministry. There are many reasons that the Lord may send someone on a mission. Each apostle will receive his direction from the Holy Spirit and it will involve various functions from others who are also called as apostles.

An apostle hears what the Spirit is saying to the churches and sets order accordingly for the growth and maturity of the church. Setting order, as Chief Apostle, also entails the function of a mediator between other apostles. As I continue to function in this capacity, I am aware that mediation will only be pleasing to the Lord, when its course of action is done *decently and in order,* according to 1 Corinthians 14:40.

Apostles need, on a continuum, vital components to keep Ministry alive. The following are most important to an apostle's mission as overseer of the church:

A. Positive relationship with prophets

(2 Chronicles 20:20; St. John 14:26)

B. Personal intercessors

(Romans 8:26-27; St. John 14:26)

C. Recognition and affirmation

(Hebrews 2:1-4; Titus 1:1-4)

D. Communication channels must remain open

(Titus 3; Titus 1:1-4).

E. Functional accountability

(I Peter 2:13-14; 2 Peter 2:8-22)

You can discern a true apostle by the fruit they bear, for every tree is known by its own fruit (Luke 6:44). The 12 Apostles laid the foundation for the early church to be established. They were mandated to share with others what they had experienced with the Messiah, which was the "Good News," the plan of redemption and reconciliation. As we know from history, the Apostles did fulfill their assignment by establishing the early church and mentoring both men and women to carry on the work.

Accountability and responsibility are mandates to which we must aspire. God's Apostolic Woman has been entrusted with His Mission and those of us who have accepted His Calling must be willing to hear His Voice and obey His Word. How can I truly fulfill

God's predestined plan for my life, when I do not seek to connect with His Purpose and carry out the Mission that He established, before I was formed in my mother's womb?

Apostles have divine authority which is activated within a divine sphere. I am required and expected to exhibit an authoritative demeanor and diligence within the limits of the sphere in which God has appointed, for the edification of the body of Christ. The Bible admonishes us to *walk worthy of the vocation wherewith ye have been called (Ephesians 4:1).* I have listed below 10 characteristics that must be in operation of a true apostle of Christ:

1. **Apostles of Christ Build the Kingdom**
   Apostles of Christ have an ambassadorial call that transcends any one church, movement, or denomination. God constantly pulls them into other church communities and/or nations to build apostolic foundations related to doctrine or kingdom life. The Apostolic Woman is graced, anointed to build His Kingdom.

2. **Apostles of Christ are not Hierarchical**
   Apostles of Christ do not personally crave titles (they will use them when appropriate) and do not need institutional church structures to validate their

ministry or calling. The Apostolic Woman needs His Validation. Man's praise is often swayed by feelings or emotions, which are temporal and can be fictitious.

3. **Apostles of Christ do not Strive for Recognition**

Philippians 2 teaches us that Jesus made Himself of no reputation. Apostles of Christ are often hidden and do not seek public attention, since they are already rooted strongly in their identity as sons of God. "What you see is what you get!" I am not ashamed of being transparent before God's people! The Apostolic Woman seeks recognition and approval from the Lord.

4. **Apostles of Christ are not Driven by Money**

Apostles of Christ have great faith in their assignment from God; their trust is girded in the belief that God will provide all their needs if they are in His will. They do not go to a place to minister, to peddle the Word of God because the offerings are good, but will go only where the Lord is leading (2 Corinthians 2:17).

5.   **Apostles of Christ Lay Down their Lives for the Gospel**

All the original 12 apostles (except John) were martyred for the gospel. As Jesus laid down His life for the sheep (John chapter 10), those who represent Him are willing to die daily (Rev. 12:11; Acts 20:24; Gal. 2:19-20) whether it is to their own will or literally to lose their lives.

6.   **Apostles of Christ have a Servant's Heart**

Apostles of Christ do not have an entitlement mentality but have a servant's heart. They mimic Jesus' words when He said that the greatest in the Kingdom is the one who serves (Mark 10:43-45).

7.   **Apostles of Christ have Divine Influence & Calling Beyond their Network of Churches**

Since Apostles of Christ represent the Lord, by nature, they have to be trans-national, trans-cultural, and multi-generational and have a desire for kingdom advancement, not just the enlargement of their church networks.

8.   **Apostles of Christ have an Intimate Walk with God**

Since Apostles of Christ have to

represent Jesus, they are obligated to know God intimately and walk in His presence and power. All true Apostles of Christ will have a driving passion to know God and to make Him known.

9. **Apostles of Christ Endure Great Hardship**
    Apostles of Christ must have the capacity for high-stress leadership combined with the kind of emotional maturity to deal with all kinds of difficulties that the average person could not endure.

10. **Apostles of Christ Live in Simplicity**
    Apostles of Christ do not need or desire to live a life of extreme luxury. Their greatest desire in life is to fellowship with Him, meditate on the scriptures, and serve God's people.

As the Apostolic Woman, I have been called to the Office of Apostle, and I take my assignment seriously, for it is not about title or financial gain. It is truly about building the Kingdom of God. I have great compassion for Ministry. With the heart of a servant, my desire is to witness healing and deliverance for God's people, for souls to be set free, and to advance the Kingdom. Therefore, I must remain humble, for I will receive exaltation from the

Lord, in due season.

CHAPTER TWO

5 *W'S* OF AN APOSTLE

Who **is an Apostle?** The etymology of the term, "Apostle," originates from Biblical reference as any one of the 12 followers of Jesus Christ who were chosen by Him to preach the news of Christianity. An apostle is a chosen vessel of God, sent out to set order in the body of Christ. They have been anointed for the office and operate in their graces to be effective in different spheres.

An apostle is the authoritative figure of the 5-fold ministry and one who is in relationship with the One who sent him/her. The 5-fold structure is the core of "total ministry." The Apostle's purpose is to govern, the Prophet is to guide, the Evangelist is to gather, the Pastor is to guard, and the Teacher is to ground.

What **is the primary role**? Some of the key roles of an apostle are to exercise discipline and bring correction. This role is the key component to bringing order to the body of Christ. It is the apostle who sets order by example and using wisdom. This is one area where the apostle will rely heavily on the leading of the Holy Ghost. Being in a leadership position, many who will follow may express differing views, but it is the Office of the Apostle who has been charged to set order.

Apostles must be custodians of sound doctrine. During the time when Jesus walked the earth, He exposed erroneous teaching that continually tried to penetrate God's people and cause them to stray from real purpose and God's plan. God has always raised up men and women to stand for righteousness and rightly divide the word of truth, according to 2 Timothy 2:15. The people of God have always needed guidance when it comes to the things of God. Although we have the Holy Ghost today, we still need apostles to stand for God's truth.

Apostles bring balance, strengthen churches, protect and foster relationships, provide vision and safety, prepare God's people for good work, provide exposure to Christ in other churches, hold leading pastors accountable, and offer continued leadership training.

These Traits Make Apostles Different:

1. They have a spiritual gift (1 Corinthians 12:28).
2. They have an assignment or a mission to fulfill (1 Corinthians 12:26).
3. They possess and exhibit extraordinary character (James 3:1; 1 Corinthians 12:28).
4. They have voluntary and grateful followers.
5. They have vision (2 Corinthians 12:1).

Why is it important to understand? It is important to understand how the Office of the Apostle operates in the 5-fold ministry that was established by Jesus. *And he gave some apostles...*this statement alone verifies that God gave credence to appointing the apostle to establish and oversee the work in the Kingdom of God. Many in the body of Christ have challenges in following order. Yes, when we are filled with the Holy Ghost, we are endowed with power from God. It is also true that as you form relationship with God, He does speak to us individually. God has strategically placed leaders over His people to oversee and make sure that His plan is fulfilled.

The Bible says, in Isaiah 55:11, *So shall my word be that goeth forth out of my mouth; it shall not return unto me void, but it shall accomplish that which I please, and it shall prosper in the thing whereto I sent it.* God has proven Himself to be a God of order from the beginning of time. As the world was created by the spoken word of God, so are His chosen vessels placed by the same spoken word. To only accept part of God's instructions would be the same as trying to separate God from His word.

When was it established? It is indisputable in saying that Jesus was the first established Apostle to walk among us. He was given instructions from the Father to come to earth and re-establish order.

Where can you find the origin of the Apostle?
Wherefore, holy brethren, partakers of the heavenly calling, consider the Apostle and High Priest of our profession, Jesus Christ (Hebrew 3:1). The first Apostle mentioned in the Bible is Jesus; He was appointed over God's entire house. The Father sanctified Jesus and sent Him into the world (John 10:36). This is from where the word Apostle is derived. The Father delegated His responsibility and authority to His son and sent Him as a representative or Apostle to build God's church (Hebrew 3:1-5).

Jesus now chooses certain men and delegates His authority and responsibility to them, so that they might represent Him to the church and build the church through the grace He has given to them.

The first 12 men whom God chose to be apostles had a very special apostolic calling. They were to be witnesses of His ministry upon the earth and of His resurrection. Their qualification was that He had called them specifically to tell others about the things that Jesus did, before and after His resurrection.

Although these 12 will always be regarded as the greatest of Jesus' apostles, they are not the only apostles or the only kind of apostles who Christ would raise up and send out.

CHAPTER THREE

VISION COMES TO PASS (HABAKKUK 2:2)

When I was given the vision of Apostleship for my leader in 1983, I never imagined that God was allowing me to see a glimpse of what was to come in my own life. I was given the awesome assignment to write the vision that would thrust my pastor into the forefront. The vision revealed that Christ was the ultimate Apostle, for He was sent to represent His Father. Although the original 12 apostles had great purpose, the mantle did not stop when they transitioned from labor to reward. *Thanks be unto God* that He allowed the mantle to continue to fall so that those of us who are alive today can still partake of His glory.

*Verily, verily I say unto you, He that believeth on me, the works that I do shall he do also; and greater works that these shall he do; because I go unto my Father (*St. *John 14:12).* This scripture is evident that the mantle continues to fall on those who operate through faith-those that dare to believe God and take Him at His word. My former pastor was operating in the Office of the Apostle before he ever acknowledged the call. He was a man divinely sent and commissioned to represent Christ (Hebrews 3:1). The challenges of being called to the office alone compels you to know without uncertainty that you truly were called by God. It is more than a title. You must be able to produce.

Where the apostle goes, they must fulfill their mission to:

A. **Perform Miracles** (Matthew 10:1,8)
Behold, God has given power/authority to my servant to heal, cast out, bind, deliver and let the oppressed go free. To operate in a place of faith to believe whatsoever you speak, it shall come to pass.

B. **Preach the Gospel** (Acts 28:19-20)
When no one else can deliver the people, God sends His true apostle, for there is no place too deep or wide, good or bad, that his servant will not go.

C. **Witness Christ's Resurrection** (Acts 1:22, 10:40, 42)
Many preach Christ's death, but very few preach His resurrection. Without resurrecting power, redemption would have never taken place. The apostle preaches life into the people. They are then delivered, not by what they see, but by what they see and hear. This allows them to be free from the bondage of

death in sin.

D. **Write Scripture** (Ephesians 3:5)
Apostle's walk in revelation and it must
be written down because of the unbelief
of man that will come your way.

E. **Establish the Church** (Ephesians 2:20)
The growth of the Church lies within
the apostle's hands, under the direction
of Christ. The apostle is part of the
foundation and without their guidance,
many will be lost.

Jesus experienced some limitations while in the
earth, due to unbelief. The people were looking for a
promised Messiah who would come to save them.
However, when the promised Messiah appeared,
they missed it, for they could not accept how He
came. Surely the God of Abraham, Isaac and Jacob
would cause His promise to come in a grandeur way
that everyone would know and be in awe. Chosen
people's enemies would be destroyed and the people
would be vindicated.

Religious people missed the message that Jesus
brought, for they could not accept the messenger.
Jesus did not match the concept of the Messiah that
was established in the people's mind. Is this still an
issue today? What God gave me concerning the

Office of the Apostle, never specified male or female. It didn't contain directions on having a certain pedigree, and it was not based on any educational requirements. All God requires is that you be willing to be a servant and walk in obedience.

Revelation given by God is timeless. When I was given instructions concerning this office, it never occurred to me that these would be my same instructions. God never gives vision without making provision. I did not know that God would use me, His vessel, as a catalyst to pave the way for both men and women to follow. As I reflect on my life's experiences, my relationship with God has been strengthened and has enabled me to walk in a powerful anointing. I boast not of myself. I say, powerful, for the Spirit of God that resides on the inside makes it powerful. Acceptance of my instructions, when it was my appointed time to operate in this office, started many years ago, lying in my bed at Roseland Hospital. I gave God an unconditional, "Yes." It was that, Yes, which set me on the path that led to where I am in God on today. I recognized my purpose, yielded to my process and I *now* allow God's glory to be revealed in me.

I am on a search to find out what has happened to the spirit of Joshua? If spirits don't die but transfer, where is the spirit of Joshua in the land?

- The servant who is standing at the bottom of the mountain awaiting his leader's return
- The one standing in agreement stating, "Yes, we can possess the land."
- Obtaining the promises of God that also were given to his leader

The Lord spoke to Joshua and stated, "As I was with Moses, I shall be with you" (Joshua 1:5). Those of us in leadership must understand that it is not a head thing, it is more of a heart thing, and even more, it is a heart of God thing. I stood in the role of a servant for my pastor, not looking for elevation, but elevation came. It came, for I genuinely love God and the people of God. When you are divinely poured into…treasure what you have, for you never know when it will become your time to operate in it.

CHAPTER FOUR

KNOWING YOUR GRACE AS AN APOSTLE

And he gave some, apostles; and some, prophets; and some, evangelists; and some, pastors and teachers; For the perfecting of the saints, for the work of the ministry, for the edifying of the body of Christ (Ephesians 4:11-12).

As we are called to different offices in the body, we don't operate in that office the same, but we all are governed by the same Holy Spirit. This holds true for the Office of the Apostle. There is no "cookie cutter" form to being an apostle. Each servant, selected and chosen by God to this office, will operate in their own uniqueness. Psalm 139:14 says, *I will praise thee; for I am fearfully and wonderfully made: marvelous are thy works; and that my soul knoweth right well.* This scripture adheres to our uniqueness in both life and in God.

God only requires you to be whom He has ordained. It is amazing, when you reflect that before you were ever formed in your mother's womb God already had a plan concerning your life, and He already knew how your story was going to end.

There are many different kinds of apostles who

minister in many different spheres. At this time, I will discuss 4 types of apostles. The first type to be discussed is the vertical apostle. **The Vertical Apostle** has established a clear governmental structure, whereby all are accountable on several different levels that may include, personal, familial, within their network, and among others in the body of Christ. The word, *vertical*, is defined as *holding an upright position or straight, up and down.* Examples of vertical apostles:

- **Ecclesiastical Apostle** – Apostles who are given authority over a sphere which includes a number of churches, presumably in an apostolic network headed up by the apostle
- **Functional Apostle** – Apostles who are given authority over those who have an ongoing ministry in a certain specific sphere of service which has defined boundaries of participation
- **Apostolic Team Members** – Apostles whose apostolic functions are in conjunction with an apostle who is seen as the leader of a team of one or more other peer-level vertical apostles. They may be assigned specific spheres by the leading apostle. These are more than administrators, assistants or armor bearers.
- **Congregational Apostle** – Apostles functioning as senior pastors of dynamic, growing churches of more than 700-800 people

The second type to be discussed is the **Horizontal Apostle**. The word, *horizontal*, is defined as being *parallel, in the same direction, similar, or side by side.* Horizontal apostles have a certain relational credibility among a wide cross section of people and cultures. This standing and respect allows the horizontal apostle to summons other apostles and leaders to attend "iron sharpening iron" conferences that create relational ties. Examples of horizontal apostles:

- **Convening Apostle** – Apostles who have authority to call together on a regular basis peer-level leaders who minister in a defined field
- **Ambassadorial Apostle** – Apostles who have itinerant, frequently international ministries of catalyzing and nurturing apostolic movements on a broad scale
- **Mobilizing Apostle** – Apostles who have the authority to take leadership in bringing together qualified leaders in the body of Christ for a specific cause or project
- **Territorial Apostle** – Apostles who have been given authority for leading a certain segment of the body of Christ in a given territorial sphere such as a city or state

The third type to be discussed is the **Hyphenated Apostle**. These apostles have a defined primary function. Many apostles are "hyphenated." They are frequently hyphenated with other government offices, such as Apostle-Prophet or Pastor-Apostle.

The last to be discussed is the **Marketplace Apostle**. This is the epitome of the "church without walls." The real Church of Jesus Christ is not a building or a denomination. It is a people from every tribe, tongue and nation who have taken up their Cross to follow the Lamb wherever He leads them, even death. Since real people work and live in the marketplace and in business of everyday life, this is where real ministry should take place. Jesus is our example, and He did not build an organization, but rather He built people and met with them where they lived and carried out their day to day activities.

A church with an apostolic vision will train people up and send them out to work in the world. We are in this world but not of this world. It is our responsibility, as Believers, especially in leadership position, to expand the Kingdom. In Jesus' time, apostles were very hands involved in expanding the work of Jesus Christ. They were not located in churches being in full time ministry. They were considered marketplace apostles who were also businessmen, farmers, fishermen, military or government officials. Only relatively few people like Samuel or Ezekiel were full time priests. This would disqualify the belief that in order to be really spiritual you need to be in full time ministry.

And the lord said unto the servant, Go out into the highways and hedges, and compel them to come in, that my house may be filled (Luke 14:23). Everyone is not coming to God, on their own. There are many who need to be evangelized. Jesus was the ultimate example. He spent very little time in the temple, but he labored outside where the people lived, worked, or gathered. Wherever He went, change occurred. Some of God's best pastors will never stand behind a pulpit but will pastor their neighborhoods or their co-workers. The marketplace is the place the Lord has always desired to influence with His presence.

Apostles are actively involved in spiritual warfare. The anointing to significantly impact enemy strongholds is clearly seen throughout the scriptures and clearly indicates a sign of supernatural spiritual authority and power. Though anyone may operate in supernatural anointing, apostles regularly flow in and out of the anointing, demonstrating evangelistic, pastoral, prophetic, teaching and power gifting.

It is important to know your position in the body as Apostle. If you attempt to flow outside of your grace, you will be ineffective in the Kingdom. The anointing is not attached to the title but to the work. All true apostles will be more concerned with relationship, rather than just enforcing their authority.

CHAPTER FIVE

THE APOSTOLIC WOMAN

Who is the Apostolic Woman?

The Apostolic Woman is a Vessel chosen by God. The Apostolic Woman does not possess a prideful spirit, but she walks in the spirit of humility. Looking at her, you would never know exactly *what* "Yes," has cost her, just to be a vessel unto God and made for the Master's use. Life's experiences have taught her how to lead with a servant's heart. In spite of her elevation, she is a servant, first and foremost. Ephesians 4:1 says, *I therefore, the prisoner of the Lord beseech you that ye walk worthy of the vocation wherewith ye are called.* The Apostolic Woman is certain that she has been called by God. This is where her inner strength shines, for she has been challenged and faces much opposition. Even when the work to which God has called her has manifested before the people, they still cannot see pass her gender and will never be blessed by her anointing. The Apostolic Woman is a yielded vessel, continually seeking the voice of God and willing to obey Him, with every fiber of her being. She makes sacrifices that are rarely understood by others, especially those who walk closely with her.

The Apostolic Woman may be connected to several natural relationships such as a daughter, sister, wife, mother, grandmother, cousin, and aunt. The

Apostolic Woman perfects the art of being a multitasker by using wisdom on how to minister to herself, so that she will be effective in Ministry. We must take time to acknowledge that family is definitely an integral part of ministry. This only enhances whom God has called, for it takes strength and guidance from God to enable her to fulfill commitment unto God, while nurturing her loved ones.

Where did the Apostolic Woman come from?

And God said, Let us make man in our image, after our likeness...(Genesis 1:26). Woman is what God pulled out of man to show man what had been placed on the inside of him. The Apostolic Woman was born out of a, *"Yes,"* and an invitation of "whosoever will, let him come." She came from a place of availability and submission. Look at the body of Christ today. There is an abundance of women who are being anointed and appointed, for they have a ready, *Yes*, in their hearts to serve and obey. The Apostolic Woman has positioned herself to do the will of God despite the sacrifice involved. Man's displacement opened the door to woman's elevation, and she is saying, "Send me, I'll go!"

When does the Apostolic Woman Function?

The Apostolic Woman functions when there is a need to rise to the occasion. As we study the Bible, we see that women have always played a vital role in the kingdom of God. Often times, "she" was referred to as "a certain woman." I believe this was written in that nature to concentrate on the purpose which she was fulfilling, at that time. There are certain characteristics that God has placed in women that cause us to yield and give God a Yes! God uses our gifts and talents to enhance the kingdom of God, once we have yielded our will to His. Just because the woman has been appointed to the Office of the Apostle, she does not lose who she is in God but uses her resources to glorify God.

The Apostolic Woman functions when she is moved by the Holy Ghost. The Bible says, *He that hunger and thirst after righteousness shall be filled (Matthew 5:6).* For those that are filled with the Holy Ghost, there is a hunger to know God intimately. As you yield to the spirit of God, you will take on His attributes and you will thirst for more of God.

The Apostolic Woman functions when the vision is clear. In Judges Chapter 4, there was a prophetess by the name of Deborah who operated as a judge for the people of God. She gave clear instructions from God to Barak concerning the battle, but Barak refused to go without Deborah. Deborah was clear of the vision that the Lord had for His people, so she readily went with Barak declaring the Lord will sell Sierra over into the hand of a woman. There was an anointing on Deborah to believe the instructions of the Lord and then act on them. She could have sat and waited, but we must know and understand God's timing.

The Apostolic Woman functions when opposition is present. In the book of Esther, you will find how God's plan to use an orphan girl was strategically placed in position to deliver her people from death. This young girl caught the king's eye, and favor rested on her in the time it was needed. The enemy had a trap set, but it was overturned through the obedience of the vessel used by God.

The Apostolic Woman functions when the seed appears to be cut off. We know that seeds are needed for a harvest. In the book of Ruth, we find a woman named Naomi who lost her husband and her two sons in a foreign land. All she had left was her two daughters-in-law. Naomi decided to return home and her daughter-in-law, Ruth, would not leave her but decided to follow her mother-in-law. Naomi did not see any value in Ruth going with her, but God had another plan. God orchestrated His divine plan. Not only was her husband's seed *not cut off* but through the union of Boaz and Ruth, Obed, which was the grandfather of King David, was born.

The Apostolic Woman functions when the promise is in danger of slipping away. In II Kings Chapter 4:8, you will read about the Shunammite woman who through her obedience, petitioned her husband to allow her to make a chamber for the Prophet Elisha, when he would pass through town. *Because* of her faith unto him, the man of God wanted to bless her. It was brought to Elisha's attention that she did not have a son. Elisha spoke a word into the woman's life and she bore a son who later died of heat stroke. The Shunammite woman laid her son in Elisha's chamber and went to see the prophet. When questioned if anything was wrong, she would state, "All is well." The woman never acknowledged her son's condition. She stayed with the prophet until he returned to her home and life was placed back into her son's body.

Why does the Apostolic Woman exist?

The Apostolic Woman exists because she is necessary in the kingdom of God. To question her worth, would be to question why woman were created by God. As leaders, we are assigned to certain souls in the Kingdom. Reflect on this for a moment…Were you able to glean from every type of ministry to which you were exposed? Your answer was probably, "No," and that is acceptable. The

President of the United States is the president for all the people. However, a leader is the leader for some; one leader is not going to reach every soul.

What makes the anointing of the Apostolic Woman so unique in every area of her life?

The Apostolic Woman is unique *because* of her Creator. She is fearfully and wonderfully made; marvelous are thy works. The Apostolic Woman has a double womb, for God blessed her with the ability to bring forth life both naturally and spiritually. Looking from the spiritual aspect, after conception (which is the vision), she is committed to nurture the seed that has been entrusted in her womb, until it is ready to come to full manifestation in the earthly realm. She possesses strength in her loins to carry the vision from conception to manifestation. Naturally her body was designed to be able to protect the seed from any outside sources that may cause harm until life is prepared to be birthed out. The Apostolic Woman possesses that same ability in the spirit realm. She is committed to seeing that nothing interferes with the growth and development of the charge that she has been given by God.

CHAPTER SIX

THE MALE APOSTLE'S PERSPECTIVE

I am about building relationship and not practicing religion. During my journey, I have been blessed to have men strategically placed in my life at specific times for divine purpose. Each one that I have been blessed to form a relationship with has added to the ministry/vision that God has entrusted to me. I am honored to call them brother, friend and co-laborers in the gospel of Jesus Christ. *No man is an island* and you need to have fellow laborers who have been called to walk a similar path that you have been ordained to walk.

I was honored to be able to capture the views of three of my fellow co-laborers who are male apostles. The interviews are evidence that God uses whomever he chooses and it is never based on gender. This book is not being penned to display women as trying to be superior to men, but to open man's understanding that in the eyes of God, all He sees is *servant.* Isn't it ironic that the One, *Who* created gender, is not concerned about it, when purpose must be fulfilled? All He is requiring is a willing vessel. I thank God for those who can rightly interpret the scripture through the Holy Ghost. These three men of God have walked with me at different times during my journey as an Apostolic Woman.

Apostle Virgil Jones was consecrated to the Office of Apostle on November 12, 2013.

It is never about titles but it is about the work. Apostle Jones was doing the work before he ever accepted his assignment formally. In my journey, my prayer has been, "Lord, surround me with folks that simply love you and desire to walk in the spirit of obedience." Apostle Virgil Jones has demonstrated a life that reflects his desire to please God. Apostle Jones is an advocate for servants to be used in the kingdom of God, to enhance it at all cost. Some women apostles may try harder to prove themselves, for they are challenged with opposition. Ultimately, God calls whom He wants.

Apostle Jones spoke about his first experience when speaking with me stating, "The Holy Spirit revealed to me that you were a Chief Apostle without even knowing that you were a pastor, when we first met." Emphasis was placed on the Holy Ghost, revealing it to the man of God. Apostle Jones encourages the apostolic woman to stand in her calling, obey, and seek direction from God, not people. This is important because you are responsible for governing God's people, which requires you to stay before the Lord, so you can hear the voice of God. Apostle Jones shared that one of the challenges you face in this office is when a leader is out of the will of God. You must rebuke them and restore them. It hurts to see leaders fall. A scripture he lives by is I Peter 1:16, *Because it is written, Be ye holy; for I am holy.* God wants us to be like Him.

Apostle Jones spoke a word to my mother, Elder Louise Lee-Snipes, who was a widow after 54 years of marriage to my father, Carl Lee Sr. He told her that she would marry, again. She married Deacon Charles Snipes of Fairmont, West Virginia. My stepfather most recently went to be with the Lord, but thank you for my mother having a companion with whom she could share the word of God daily. He loved her just because…Apostle Jones is kingdom minded, focused and centered. I praise God for this man of God who gave me the second seed for our new church. Praise God! You are in Chicago to bless His people!

Apostle Robbie C. Peters was consecrated to apostleship, 15 years ago.

Apostle Peters revealed, "I am an advocate for them and Mark chapter 16 supports my views." Women continue to be on the scene, standing in the gap and instrumental in the furtherance of the Gospel of Jesus Christ. Women have taken on roles needed because there was no man to do it. Due to the opposition they face, they need people around them that are trustworthy and can help them steer the ship. Surround themselves with people that walk in integrity and don't try to push them outside of their grace.

I believe it is important to have a male presence to discourage opportunities of taking advantage in certain settings. Apostle Peters defined "Chief Apostle" as one who oversees several apostles known as "reformation." Some religious people would argue that Jesus was the "only Chief Apostle." I would like to encourage the woman apostle. "Continue to stand in your walk, never compromise and always obey God." Remember to operate in your grace and not your gender. One of the challenging areas is not knowing who you are in God, which will cause you to operate outside of the office. Apostles are travelers; Pastors stay home and oversee the church. I live by 1 Thessalonians 4:11, *And that ye study to be quiet, and to do your own business, and to work with your own hands, as we commanded you.*

Apostle Robbie C. Peters and Apostle Sharon Peters, my brother and sister are great examples of change agents. They are truly a blessing to the body of Christ. Apostle Robbie C. Peters is the father of order when it comes to the kingdom of God. This man of God has given ceaselessly to the Kingdom. I just want to say, "Thank you, for never giving up on the people of God. You and Apostle Sharon keep allowing God to bless and teach God's chosen vessels."

Chief Apostle Sylvester Paul Brinson III

This man of God believes, "There is no such thing as a woman apostle." Apostle Brinson stands on Galatians 3:28, *There is neither Jew nor Greek, there is neither bond nor free, there is neither male nor female: for ye are all one in Christ Jesus.* My view is God's view. He doesn't discriminate in gender; we are one in the same in God's eyes. A support system is needed to understand that they are equal when it comes to the dispensation of the gifts in the spirit. They are not second class citizens and are used just as much in the building of the kingdom of God.

Women should support one another, but sometimes they display the most opposition in submission. Even through opposition, remain faithful to the call. Apostle Brinson defined, *Chief Apostle*, as an Apostle who is responsible for the tutelage of other apostles or a senior apostle who has other apostles submitting to their leadership-fathering under their spiritual watch care sons/daughters, enhancing spiritual relationship and covering. Out of this develops fellowship, alliance and networking. The position of a chief apostle represents respect, honor, and responsibility, as opposed to hierarchy. Jesus washed the disciples' feet. *But he that is greatest among you shall be your servant (Matthew 23:11).*

I encourage the apostolic woman to understand that she has been called by God. To present her body as a living sacrifice. Submit to the giver of the gift and not the receivers. You must know that you are called and submit to the Holy Ghost who will teach you. Learn to celebrate the call that has been placed on you. The greatest challenge an apostle faces are principalities and spiritual warfare. You must learn how to navigate in the spirit realms. An apostle is called to set order, strengthen and lay foundation in God's kingdom. When you come against the spirit of religion, spiritual warfare is inevitable. I live by Romans 12:1, *I beseech you therefore brethren, by the mercies of God, that ye present your bodies a living sacrifice, holy, acceptable unto God, which is your reasonable service.*

Apostle Sylvester Paul Brinson III, the words of purpose and promise spoken to my daughter, Prophet Taneshia R. Lee, has changed my life and the Body of Christ. Man of God, thank you for wisdom, knowledge and destiny, and for allowing the Body of Christ Seminary and Bible Institute to be a part of the kingdom of God. Thank you for the Apostolic round table where the apostles can come together to get educated and fellowship, so that we can keep standing. Praise God for Lady Brinson, the dancer, chef, administrator and voice of reason to all who will receive! We do eat well spiritually and naturally at Brinson Institute. Keep the vision moving forward.

CHAPTER SEVEN

12 VOICES OF THE APOSTOLIC WOMAN

After interviewing several women apostles, it is quite evident through listening to them share their story, each were chosen of God to do the work of an apostle. The criteria of an apostle is one that has been sent to build and oversee the work of the ministry as it pertains to Kingdom building.

The woman apostle is challenged. Although she is fully persuaded that she has been chosen by God to do the work, she still must constantly overcome obstacles to make sure that she carries out her assignment as God has designed. Each of these women has one common denominator and that is whether accepted or not, they know that they are called of God. Each woman of God shared some of their experiences since they were called to the Office of Apostle. I want to share how they have impacted my life through divine connection.

Chief Apostle JoAnna Bean
Consecrated on October 28, 2006

Chief Apostle JoAnna Bean has been my spiritual mom, for over 30 years. She has poured into me and my family members and transformed our lives. Chief Apostle Bean gave me sound wisdom and knowledge.

This vessel has been greatly used by God. One night, after preaching, my ankle that was challenged many years ago, a blood vessel broke. This woman of God laid hands on my ankle praying the prayer of faith and I was made whole. I share such rich history with Chief Apostle JoAnna Bean.

The Real Woman of God Fellowship started in my home and then in the basement of her church. She has been a pillar, anchor, confidant, prayer warrior, teacher, exhorter and most of all, wise counsel. The word of God is her source and strength. She refuses to do without it. She doesn't compromise with the devil. This woman of God is 80+ years old, possessing a sound mind and still declares that Jesus is her choice. I love and respect her for being a woman of faith, power in my life as well as my family. I will always remember her words to me. "Always obey God and let nothing or no one stop you from serving Him with all your heart." *Refer to Ephesians 3:20.*

Chief Apostle Bean displays much wisdom and maturity when it comes to the things of God. There rests a heavy anointing on Chief Apostle Bean which graces her to make great impartations into other men and women of God. Apostle Bean shares that her greatest experience was when God allowed her to become Chief Apostle, placing churches and ministries under her leadership for guidance.

Although it was her greatest experience, it also came with its challenges.

"Being a Chief Apostle, you have many personalities to contend with from other ministries. Everyone who says they love you, don't love you. You must deal with that and continue to love them. You must use wisdom during the times you are in fellowship." The golden nugget, which Chief Apostle Bean would give to the future woman apostle is, "There are many challenges. so you must be sure you have been called by God. People think it is such a grand life in being an apostle and many have not been called. When you have been called by God, much fasting and praying is needed to maintain the position. It is the fasting and praying that exposes the false teachers and false prophets. Be led by God, for you are who He has called to minister to His people. The word of God is how I live. It is my source." Acts 17:28 says, *For in him we live, and move, and have our being; as certain also of your own poets have said, For we are also his offspring.*

Apostle Denise Clark
House of Rhema Praise & Worship Center
Consecrated 16 years

Apostle Denise Clark was my hair stylist, and she

rose up early to do my hair. As she did my hair, I would share with her about God and how he had a calling on her life for ministry. I knew her mother's pastor, Rev. Rucker, before I met her family. Apostle Clark loves to worship and praise God. Apostle Clark can sing until the glory of God is revealed. However, she would run from being called to the Office of Pastor. Praise God, she finally said, "Yes," Lord! She received wise counsel from many. Later the Lord elevated her again to Apostle Dr. Denise Clark. Twenty years later, we are still connected *because* of her, *Yes.*

As a true worshipper, Apostle Dr. Denise Clark understands the importance of being in the presence of God. Apostle Denise Clark is doing the work in my singleness. This woman of God shares that her greatest experience as being an apostle is seeing deaf ears and blinded eyes opened. "A family came to Chicago from Ohio to be in a service with Pastor Benny Hinn. The son got separated from the family, so they never made it to the service. The mom brought the family to my church. Just before they came, I told the Lord that I needed to see blinded eyes open and deaf ears unstopped. Right there in the service, the son received his sight and hearing." Apostle Clark shares, "If you activate your faith, God will do the rest."

Apostle Clark stated that her greatest challenges are ministering to the millennial, for at times, they are hard converts. This is due to them being exposed to so many things like social media and other avenues of modern technology. This challenges their faith to be in operation and makes it difficult for them to become Believers. Apostle Denise Clark leaves these words of wisdom to the upcoming woman apostle, "Make your calling and election sure" (2 Peter 1:10). "People don't readily accept apostles; especially for women apostles, the road is more difficult. If you have been called, then stay with it. Too many people are starting and then stop. Stay in the press, it is not an easy job and sometimes it can be lonely. That is why you must know that you have been called by God. Competition and jealousy can surface because people are intimidated by your strength." John 4:24 says, *God is a Spirit and they that worship him must worship him in spirit and in truth.*

Apostle Linda C. Shearrill
It's all about the Souls International Deliverance Outreach Ministry
Consecrated in 2015

My baby daughter, Tarina, transitioned August 12, 2003. She had been sick, since 1999, but God kept her and performed many miracles for her; she received a new heart and new kidney. However, the Father still called her home. Apostle Shearrill prayed and fasted with me during this time. When she became Bishop, I was compelled to support the work on August 15, 2003. It didn't stop there because life events continued to happen. The woman of God became an apostle at a time when my brother transitioned, and I still supported her. No matter what happens, the kingdom of God is what truly makes me happy. This woman of God, her church and my spiritual daughter and co-pastor, Cynthia Eubanks, are truly advancing the Kingdom nationally and internationally. They live by Luke 10:19 and Luke 18:1.

For Apostle Linda C. Shearrill, it has always been about the souls of men. Apostle Shearill has been in ministry for 48 years. She shared that she has been doing the work of an Apostle for a long time. Apostle Henton consecrated her as Bishop, in 2003, because when she went to foreign countries it was more acceptable. Her greatest experience is when souls get saved, healed and delivered. "My main goal is soul winning. I have witnessed miracles of healing. In the Philippines, God used me to open blinded eyes and deaf ears unstopped. My greatest challenge is having the resources needed to go minister the gospel to different places because it takes money. The Lord has always provided miracles for me. I walk by faith. I do crusades by faith. Sometimes I only buy a ticket one way or pay for one night at the hotel, and God has always made provisions for me. I encourage the future woman apostle to remain faithful to the Lord. Be a humble servant and sold out to Jesus. Give 100% to God and fulfill the work of the Lord. Let, *Yes Lord,* be the core of your existence." Luke 10:19 says, *Behold I give unto you power to tread on serpents and scorpions, and over all the power of the enemy: and nothing shall by any means hurt you.*

Apostle Deborah Alexander
Promoting A New Mindset
Stedfast Love Global Inc.
Consecrated in 2007

Apostle Deborah Alexander received her charge at the Real Woman of God Fellowship in Chicago. This woman of God is passionate about souls. She is known for bringing women from all over to receive what God has for them at the fellowship. Apostle Alexander lives in Georgia and is doing an awesome work to advance the kingdom of God.

This woman of God's mission is to promote a new mindset for the people of God. Apostle Alexander shared that one of her greatest experience is to speak into the lives of God's people and impart ministry ideas that God has given. Her greatest challenge is the status quo of organized religion or getting the people of God to move past ideology of the past. For example, church used to be a program, now trying to get away from church as usual. "It can be challenging when people don't understand the moving of the Holy Ghost. We must allow the Holy Ghost to move in our midst. I encourage the upcoming woman apostle to be open to the creativity of the move of God's spirit. God is not one dimensional. He is multi-dimensional. There is a world waiting to be won." St. John 3:16 says, *For God so loved the world, that he gave his only begotten Son, that whosoever believeth in him should not perish, but have everlasting life.*

Apostle Bridget Outlaw
New Global Destiny International World Deliverance Ministries
Consecrated on June 10, 2010

Apostle Bridget Outlaw is an international woman of great wisdom and knowledge. She is always willing to assist anyone who needs help. She has come out to train the leaders at the Body of Christ on: Church Safety as well as Entrepreneurship. This woman of God came to Gatley Park in Roseland to help feed families. No job is too big or too small. She also took pampers to the pregnant and parenting program at the Jadonal Ford Center because I asked her for free. She is a blessing to the nation. Being part of my life to help advance the kingdom is what makes us obey His word. Truly she lives by 2 Timothy 2:15.

Apostle Bridget Outlaw is committed to showing God's people a more excellent way. Apostle Outlaw loves the God she serves and she is very committed to her assignment in the kingdom of God. She truly believes that knowledge is power. She has been equipped as an educator to the body of Christ. Apostle Outlaw shares that her greatest experience is when she is training the 5-Fold in how to serve the body of Christ. "A lot of people are not being trained in this area." Apostle Outlaw reveals that she is greatly challenged when the Office of Apostle is disrespected. "I find that churches are so bias and they celebrate and promote male apostles. The office of the apostle is not a gender but a universal role."

Future woman apostle, I leave you with these words, "Be confident in who you are before you accept the role of an apostle because this is a tough job. You won't make it with self-esteem issues. Just do the work and be passionate about the body of Christ growing and building a good foundation. I pour into others because someone poured into me." Philippians 1:6 says, *Being confident of this very thing, that he which hath begun a good work in you will perform it until the day of Jesus Christ.*

Apostle Dr. Heidi Ellis
Fresh Anointing Ministries
Consecrated 2008

Apostle Dr. Heidi Ellis is an educator, teacher, sister, mother, preacher, exhorter, etc. I have been blessed to teach at Fresh Anointing Bible College. What great wisdom and knowledge that has been given to her by God to save souls and empower leaders to be leaders!

Apostle Christopher Ellis, thank you for the introduction of this awesome woman of God. This opened up a door for my daughter, Prophet Dr. Taneshia Lee to have a spiritual father. Apostle Heidi, thank you. Keep standing, for the kingdom of God needs you.

Apostle Dr. Heidi Ellis is anointed to help souls get healed delivered and made free. She is used by God to reveal in order to be healed. Apostle Heidi Ellis shares that her greatest experience was the interaction she has experienced with male clergy. "There are times when they are accepting or not accepting of women apostles. I have learned to adjust to the place they are in at that time. My greatest challenge is the burden I have for God's people. I asked to supply my needs but move the carnality of material things and teach me how to labor with the people. God allows me to hear and see what they don't tell. I really labor and travail with people."

Apostle Ellis leaves Proverbs 3:6, *In all thy ways acknowledge him, and he shall direct thy paths.* "We need the Lord in everything-economically, socially, prophetic, apostolic. You need his guidance in it. Find your place, get in your place, stay in your place, and go with God. You need His guidance because every good door is not a God door. You can't lead if you don't know how to follow. Know who you are in second place, before you move to #1. Leave earthly things to be able to line up with spiritual blessings."

Scripture: Mark 10:29

And Jesus answered and said, Verily I say unto you, There is no man that hath left house, or brethren, or sisters, or father, or mother, or wife, or children or lands for my sake and the gospel's...

Apostle Frances Townsend
Spirit of Truth Full Gospel Church

Consecrated in 2011

Apostle Frances Townsend is a woman of great faith. I have known this woman of God for over 40 years. My family greatly admired her and my mother encouraged me to fellowship with her. The Lord blessed us with a great relationship and we began to advance the kingdom of God together.

Many have come and gone through her ministry; however, on the day the Lord allowed me to consecrate her as the Apostle of Spirit of Truth Full Gospel Church, people came from all over the world to witness this elevation. It was standing room only. This woman of God is the preacher's preacher and can bring souls in to be saved by her spoken word. Apostle Townsend and I ordained her son, Minister Angelo Townsend, who is my spiritual son. He continues to stand by his mother's side.

Apostle Frances Townsend testimony is prayer mixed with faith works. This is one servant who understands that application of the word will cause manifestations to flow in your life and through the ministry. She shares that her greatest experiences have included: consecrating many apostles, pastors and establishing churches, setting up ministries, broadcasting, and traveling to preach the Gospel of Christ-allowing God to use her to open doors through revival for other ministers especially for women pastors to spread the gospel. "I have never been rejected in church bringing forth the word of God."

Apostle Townsend shares that her greatest challenge is keeping the ministry operating under financial challenges. In 30 years, God has always kept the doors opened. Apostle Townsend She believes in miracles. "I encourage those women apostles of the future to stand on the word of God, obey, pray, keep faith, and endure the challenges. Everything you do, let it be done in faith by the word of God and stand! If He said it, He will perform it. Above all, keep the faith!" Now *faith is the substance of things hoped for, the evidence of things not seen (Hebrews 11:1).*

Apostle Charlene Benson
Home of Life Christian Ministry
Consecrated in 2016

Apostle Charlene Benson has been part of the Real Woman of God Fellowship for over 30 years. We started the ministry in my living room at home. Apostle Charlene Benson has transitioned a daughter, so she were able to help me in the time of my daughter's transition. Apostle Charlene was ordained pastor and apostle by way of the Holy Ghost and Apostle Dr. Yvonne Lee-Wilson. This woman is amazing and faithful. She meets all the requirements of advancing the kingdom of God.

Apostle Charlene Benson knows what it takes to walk in love. *For many are the afflictions of the righteous, but the LORD delivereth him out of them all (Psalm 34:19).* Apostle Benson identifies her greatest experience is being new to the office of Apostle. She also shares the spiritual change she has experienced since operating in the Office. Her greatest challenge has been people accepting me as an apostle. "Some people refuse to seek God for revelation and stay stuck in their own thinking pattern. I share three components with the new woman apostle: 1) Know who you are in the Lord. I encourage you to stand on *that,* regardless of what comes against you. 2) Be secure. 3) Obey what God says. *Behold, to obey is better than sacrifice (1 Samuel 15:22) .*

Apostle Verdale Sheldon
Living Sacrifice Ministries
Consecrated 20+ years

Apostle Verdale Sheldon was my teacher in college and she is an amazing woman of God. This woman of God has taught many saints of God, worked in leading hospitals and has stood on the front line as a general in the kingdom of God. Test and trials only came to strengthen you for your next dimension in the kingdom of God.

Apostle Verdale Sheldon believes in igniting the fire. Her greatest experience is witnessing the deliverance in people who have been bound and captive and showing people how to utilize freedom in Christ. I love to see the people obtain and maintain their deliverance. Apostle Verdale Sheldon's greatest challenge is breaking through the status quo-breaking the traditions of habit and familiarity in the ministry, to deliver newness and freshness to those who have become stale.

"Apostolic woman, know your purpose and understand it comes from no one except God. Emulate only him and be only like him. Hear God and God only." *Beloved, now are we the sons of God, and it doth not yet appear what we shall be: but we know that, when he shall appear, we shall be like him; for we shall see him as he is (I John 3:2).*

Apostle Vee Robinson
Anointed House of Prayer
Consecrated in 2007

Apostle Vee Robinson is the revelator of the apostles. This woman of God has prayer every morning and noonday. She will travel all across the nation to win souls for the kingdom of God. Apostle Vee Robinson is a friend that will love at all times. Apostle Robinson takes care of all lost sheep and restores them back to health. She loves family and stands on the word of God, no matter what comes her way. "Signs, wonders and miracles do follow her, as the *Believer* in Christ Jesus."

Apostle Vee Robinson is one who is equipped to bridging the gap between adults and youth. God has gifted her to be able to relate to our youth but not compromise the standards of holiness given by God. Apostle Vee Robinson enjoys ministering to people from all walks of life. She shared her greatest experience establishing services in a senior building twice a week. Apostle Robinson states, "It has been a real blessing because others come in from outside as well as the seniors and we are doing real ministry."

"My greatest challenge is that some men pastors from different organizations believe in women pastors but won't acknowledge you. I have been viewed as intimidating and sometimes out-preaching other preachers." Apostle Robinson is a servant who does what she has been commissioned to do by God.

My advice to the future women apostle, "Stay focused, trust God and watch Him bring you through. Follow His instructions and He will bless!" My motto is Luke 18:1, *Men ought always to pray, and not to faint.*

Apostle Saundra Yancy
Consecrated in July, 2016

I knew this woman of God's husband, Marvin Yancy, who sang, "God's going to take away your heavy load." This woman of God has impacted my life because of her faith in God. I was part of her elevation as an apostle and humility was all over her. Apostle Yancy truly loves the people of God with true compassion. She embraced me as a sister and we have developed a kingly relationship. She received a leadership award in 2017 through our organization, WECE (Women Empowered for Civic Engagement) because of the work she had done. This woman of God encourages so many when she speaks and is an example to men and women in the kingdom of God. She believes and lives by Psalm 23:1, *The Lord is my shepherd; I shall not want.*

Apostle Saundra Yancy grew up in a traditional church; however, she is on a mission to "breaking the traditional." Apostle Yancy is concerned about the souls of men. She is family oriented and gives God glory that her family respects the anointing on her life. Apostle Yancy is very supportive of the ministry. She also walks in authority and respect, and her family submits to her leadership by way of the Holy Ghost. Apostle Yancy expresses the area where she has encountered challenges, which is making sure people respect the position. She states, "Respect is earned not given. Therefore you must stand your ground and demand it."

"As God elevates, maintain your Christian integrity because you will be tried in these areas by both male and female. Be secure in who you are and what God has called you to do. It's alright to be humbled but not weak. Cry and seek God for guidance because they will try to break you down. Also, to maintain boundaries letting females know I am not your *sister girl* and assuring males that I am not trying to rule over them. However, I am the vessel that God has chosen to lead them. Above all remain a lady. You can't be all to everyone."

"The experience I would like to share is about a little girl, 3 years old. Every time I would take the pulpit, her face lit up! One day, the little girl's mother came to church because she had to see who this woman was that her daughter would try to tell her about. It doesn't take a lot for me and I was humbled by this experience. The fact that I can make an impact on her life as a baby…kingdom building excites me! I knew there was a mandate on my life at an early age. My Uncle prophesied to me saying that I would never be a worldly person and he spoke into my life. I was consecrated as Apostle, in 2016, but I had been walking in the Office, since my elevation as Pastor, in 2008.

"Words of wisdom that I would like to pass on to the upcoming woman apostle are: *Be who God called you to be.* It is alright to admire but don't mimic or compete. Learn to go at your own speed and work in your own vineyard. Cultivate your own fruit and don't get nervous when it seems like it is not working, just keep working it. There is a scripture for every season in your life. A few of mine that I stand on are: Philippians 1:6; Psalm 118:17; Isaiah 59:19 and Psalm 37:25."

Chief Apostle Katherine Miles
House of Hope Ministries
Consecrated Apostle 2003
Consecrated Chief Apostle 2017

Chief Apostle Miles. truly the Lord has saved a seat for you and all the souls you have prayed and fasted *for*... You are a teacher of teachers and a prophet to the nations. Giving up is never an option, keep trusting God for those that are joined to the living, for there is hope. Thank you for allowing the Spirit of God to consecrate you as a chief apostle, with the permission of your spiritual father and apostle's permission. The Bible tells us to respect and submit to each other. Keep doing the work and know that your labor is not in vain.

Chief Apostle Katherine Myles is living proof that experiencing betrayal, "didn't break me!" This woman of God shared that her experience has been positive and she generally gets along with men. She has faced challenges while shepherding couples. She has faced opposition, due to her singleness. "Also, people try to belittle you and make you feel small. You must be confident in the vocation that you have been called. Never allow anyone to make you feel inferior. Don't be equal to man because God made them the head. As a vessel chosen by God, you must know your calling and purpose. I find refuge in Psalm 37:1; James 4:7 and Habakkuk 2:2."

Each of these vessels continue to impact the kingdom of God in a great way! Through their trials, they remain triumphant! Their gifts make room for them and bring them before great men. "Continue to stand my sister and fellow laborers in the gospel. The Father that sees in secret will reward you openly. I am blessed to have relationship and fellowship with each of you. We, as Apostolic Women, will remain faithful to the assignment to advance the kingdom of God."

CHAPTER EIGHT

MINISTRY BEGINS WITH ME

The English idiom **"don't judge a book by its cover"** is a metaphorical phrase which means "you shouldn't prejudge the worth or value of something, by its outward appearance alone." People see the glory but they don't know my story. They can't even image what my, *Yes!*, to God cost me. I am not complex; there are just a lot of details that make up who I am. We place a lot of emphasis on gifts, callings, and ministry. However, we sometimes fail to realize that we must experience wholeness in every part of our lives. Jesus came to minister unto the whole man.

A **holistic view** means that we are interested in engaging and developing the whole person. You can think of this as different levels: Physical, emotional, mental and spiritual. I believe in ministering to the whole needs of man and it started with myself. In order for me to be effective in the kingdom of God, I needed to be well rounded and grounded. Not afraid to experience life but rooted in God's plan for my life. I realize that God didn't just want a part of me (my Sunday's best) but he wanted all of me. He was the only one that showed me love that was truly unconditional. Through my own personal experiences, I discovered that in order to reach a place of real healing in God, I would have to be active in my own process. There had to be a balance in my life. *And* *the LORD God formed man of the dust of the ground, (body) and breathed into his nostrils the breath of life; (spirit) and man became a living soul Genesis 2:7).* This scripture identifies the importance of having balance in our lives.

God is concerned about our mind. This is a place where peace is to abide. So how do I cleanse my mind? I continually find myself in a place of meditation, where I am seeking His face. I have the power to plant or dismiss over what stays in my mind, according to II Corinthians 10:4-5: *For the weapons of our warfare are not carnal, but mighty through God to the pulling down of strong holds; Casting down imaginations, and every high thing that exalteth itself against the knowledge of God, and bringing into captivity every thought to the obedience of Christ.* How do I take care of my mind? I am a true worshipper. I enter into His gates with thanksgiving and into his courts with praise! I believe that there are two times when you give God praise: When you feel like it and when you don't. I wrap my mind in the word of God. I spend quiet time with God to see what He is saying concerning my life. I find myself in a place of release when I do things that bring me enjoyment. I am a very family oriented person and that brings me peace and contentment. My family is five generations strong and that is rich legacy. Being a part of the second generation affords me the honor to pour into my family the knowledge and revelation that has been given to me. I have the awesome responsibility of shaping lives that are around me, so that they can be well rounded and grounded. Through my experiences, they too can learn the value of choosing life and putting God first in all things.

God is concerned about our body. *Even every one that is called by my name: for I have created him for my glory, I have formed him; yea, I have made him (Isaiah 53:7).* We were made to glorify God! I make decisions every day concerning what goes in my body; where my body will go and what my body would do. We only get one temple. I make sure that I exercise and eat right. I also have a vitamin regimen that I follow, designed for my own person needs. Yes, I am anointed! I also must take care of natural needs, so that the work that I am assigned to do is not hindered. I embrace every moment when I can make it a teachable moment. I spend time engaging in activities that bring enjoyment but also allows me to strengthen my body. I engage in physical activities (walking, tennis) and I enjoy good therapeutic massages on a regular basis. When you see me walking it out in ministry, know that I have done what I needed to do concerning my body, according to 1 Corinthians 6:19: *What? Know ye not that your body is the temple of the Holy Ghost which is in you, which ye have of God, and ye are not your own?*

God is definitely concerned about our soul. That is the essence of who you *are*. *For God sent not his Son into the world to condemn the world; but that the world through him might be saved (St. John 3:17).* We, as Believer, focus heavily on this area; however, if the other two areas are not in agreement, we will still be out of alignment with God's plan and purpose for our lives. Christians have been known to run to God to **escape our problems, hide our fears and mask our wounds**. That is what the thief wants us to do. He does not mind us coming to God, just as long as no real change/transformation occurs in the lives of men. However, you can't come into the presence of God and change not occur. The Bible says, *The thief cometh not, but for to steal, and to kill, and to destroy: I am come that they might have life, and that they might have it more abundantly (John 10:10).* He wants to **steal your promises, kill your purpose and destroy your future**. However, Christ came that you will have more than just life which is *abundant life!* Every day of my life I choose to live. It is my assignment to let others know that God is concerned about the whole man. God allowed me to tap in an area that appeared to be "taboo" in our church world, an area that would allow women to come unto him naked and unashamed.

B.A.A.D. Girls Ministry (Born Again And Delivered) is a platform for women (open to men also) to tell their stories in a nonjudgmental environment. I'm talking about saved, sanctified, tongue talking, anointed vessels who have been chosen by God, but still needed deliverance to come forth in their lives, so that they could do the work in the spirit of excellence. Your past does not care that you are on assignment from God. It is an avenue that the enemy uses to ensnare us so that we can't move fully into the promises that God has for us. God has anointed me with the grace to see pass the natural and acknowledge the treasure that is hidden in the earthly vessel. I also have a story, and it is through my experiences that allow me to identify with other like-minded Believers. By the grace and mercy of God, I didn't stay in the state of hurting but allowed God to **reveal my hurts** and was given the **opportunity to heal**. Tests that I thought would destroy me are now the testimonies that assist others with receiving deliverance. Every time I share my story with one or many, I feel blessed because I know that it is helping someone else. They see me and say, "If God did it for her, he can do it for me!" My journey was not just for me, but it was for all the lives that I would come in contact with that were hungry and waiting for change.

When I speak about coming to God, **"naked and unashamed"** it is in reference to being vulnerable and taking off the mask. In this life, change is inevitable. As a Life Coach, I walk people through "life events" to assist in the healing process, by exposing the enemy, by getting to the root cause and breaking bondages. It does not matter how long the problem has existed. Until you deal with the root cause, it will continue to manifest in some form. People need a safe place to speak freely, without being judged. They need to know that even though I am faced with some challenges, God still has a plan concerning their lives. Where they are currently is only a part of their process to get to where they need to go. You may ask, "How do I stay grounded while listening to all the challenges shared to me by others, on top of my own personal ones?" There are 4 tools which I will share to assist me in this process.

1. **Prayer**

   And he spake a parable unto them to this end, that men ought always to pray, and not to faint (Luke 18:1). **Communion with God is the key.** Prayer is a lifeline for me. When I don't know what to do, I immediately go into prayer. I am a living testimony that prayer changes things.

2. **Fasting**

    Howbeit this kind goeth not out but by prayer and fasting (Matthew 17:21. **The flesh must die.** You will never be successful in the kingdom of God, if you operate in carnality (feelings and emotions).

3. **Intercession**

    Confess your faults one to another, and pray one for another, that ye may be healed. The effectual fervent prayer of a righteous man availeth much (James 5:16). **I am my sister/brother's keeper.** You might raise the question, *"But* isn't that the same as prayer? There are times when you must really *go in,* on behalf of others. Everyone is not called to be an intercessor, but we all have the ability to intercede on the behalf of others. We just need to quiet our spirit and be open unto the leading of the Holy Ghost.

4. **Studying**

    Study to shew thyself approved unto God, a workman that needeth not to be ashamed, rightly dividing the word of truth (II Timothy 2:15). **Food for the soul** – We make sure we are full to capacity, when it comes to dealing with natural food. We eat whenever we feel hungry and sometimes when we don't. *So,* why does the body of Christ suffer from anorexia when it comes to studying and applying God's word? The **B.I.B.L.E** (Basic Instructions Before Leaving Earth) is here to guide you to all truth. I promise you, no one can deceive you, if you know what is in The Book for yourself.

God chooses to use whom He will, for He is sovereign. I am blessed because I have been able to show others a more fulfilling way to live both naturally and spiritually. God has used me as a catalyst to go through…opening doors and paving the way for others. I have ministered and poured into many souls, for the kingdom of God. What I have endured, didn't always look good or feel good, but it worked out for my good! As I continue to embrace other opportunities to mentor others, through preaching, teaching, my books, and entrepreneurship, I will continue to always give God the glory!

CHAPTER NINE

PURPOSE FOR MY PAIN

But the fruit of the Spirit is love, joy, peace, longsuffering, gentleness, goodness, faith, Meekness, temperance: against such there is no law (Galatians 5:22-23).

We fail to understand that it is our life experiences that shape us into the people we are to become. It may sound like a cliché but without a test you can't have a testimony. Tragedy breeds triumph because in God you have the victory. It is our experiences of pain that reminds us that we are still alive. As long as you are alive, you are a candidate for a miracle. *For to him that is joined to all the living there is hope: for a living dog is better than a dead lion (Ecclesiastes 9:4).* A miracle is something that you cannot explain. The Bible says, *The thief cometh not but for to steal, and to kill, and to destroy; I am come that they might have life, and that they might have it more abundantly (St. John 10:10).*

The thief or the enemy is anything or anyone that comes to detour you from God's plan for your life. The miracle is that Jesus has provided a way of escape for those of us who have entered into covenant with Him. *For I know the thoughts that I think toward you, saith the Lord, thoughts of peace, and not of evil, to give you an expected end (Jeremiah 29:11).* It is comforting to the Believer to know that I have always been on the heart and mind of God. When you really believe that God has a plan for you, the next phase is to have faith in the process that will get you to your expected end.

Remember: Anything that is worth having is worth fighting for. Out of your pain comes purpose. For everything that we experience in life there is a lesson to be learned and a blessing to receive. I know this may be difficult to digest in certain situations, but we must look for God in every situation that occurs in our lives. According to Proverbs 3:5-6, we are given specific instructions which start off by saying, *Trust in the Lord.* This is the foundation of our relationship with God. We must learn to trust Him. We have all experienced a violation of someone's trusts in some form, but we must remember that God is not a man. You must look past what your eyes see and know that God has you. This relationship with God is not a head thing but a heart of God thing.

The next part of the scripture tells us, *with all thine heart.* Here God is telling us that He wants us all in… not just in some cases but in everything. Even when you feel that the pain you are enduring is too great, God says, "Do you trust me?" In the natural, when we really love someone, we find ourselves making great sacrifices even if it hurts. God asks us, "Can you trust me from your heart?" Man's extremities are God's opportunities to get the glory. This is why we cannot go off of what we think we know.

Our finite mind can't even begin to understand the mind of God. Therefore, His instructions are to *lean not to your own understanding*. We do not have to waste your time in trying to comprehend. Just obey what the Lord orders us to do. The last part of the directions to this scripture, *In all thy ways acknowledge God and he will make your paths straight,* is a promise of God. If you consult with the Lord, He will direct your path.

Pain – A physical, mental, emotional suffering or discomfort caused by illness or injury – We want the reward of faith, but we don't want to endure the trial of faith. David said, *It was good that I have been afflicted; that I might learn thy statues (Psalm 119:71).* In essence, David was saying it was my pain that drew me to seek after you God. It was through my pain that I really learned who you are and value you as my God. How many times do we really seek after God when everything is going well in our lives?

It is those times of affliction that mature your prayer

and fasting life. When you found yourself in a situation that you knew only God could deliver, you pressed in and spent quality time with God. God's desire was always to be in relationship with His people. Sometimes pain is viewed in a negative light, but David said it was good because it reminded him of his covenant with God.

If we truly believe that God has a plan for our lives, then we would seek for the purpose of painful situations. God what are you telling or showing me? What is it that needs to change in my life? Was this pain designed to mature me and take me to my next place in you? I know what it is to experience real pain. I also have the testimony that God is a keeper, a deliverer, a restorer, a way maker, miracle worker, promise keeper and the list goes on. I learned to embrace what God has for me because I am a person with purpose. Fulfilling my purpose will take me through a process that will involve some pain.

Looking through the eyes of Jesus, I discover on the other side of pain, my destiny is waiting to unfold. God gave me a message entitled, "My Limp Has Become My Purpose." Life events that I could have allowed to cause me to give up and stumble are now the stepping stones that have positioned me in the kingdom of God today. Do not allow pain to discourage you from fulfilling your purpose. If God brings you to it, He will bring you through it.

CHAPTER TEN

REFLECTION OF MY "YES!"

When I was young, my mother, Elder Louise Lee-Snipes gave me a gift that is priceless even today. That gift was sharing with me about Jesus. Although I received the gift, it was only when I became an adult that I would I learn to cherish the gift. The motto that I live by is to *please God with every fiber of my being.*

My call to the Office of Apostle was very scary and sometimes challenging. I am very grateful that God would choose me to lead His people. I was taught by my mother that we are not better than others, we are just different. When you are different, you sometimes question the will of God. At the time that I was chosen by God, there were not a lot of women apostles. As an apostle, you must be confident in your call.

I was consecrated twice to the Office of Apostle. The first time was in 1999, when my spiritual father, Bishop Arthur M. Cofield, and my mother, Elder Louise Lee-Snipes were present to robe me and sanctioned the work. I was not concerned about having the ecclesiastic ceremony that we have today. What concerned me was the urgency to do the work. In 2003, I was consecrated, again, to the Office, because of the celebratory desires of the people under my leadership. I was later elevated to Chief Apostle, in 2008. With this elevation, the Body of Christ Reformation was birthed out.

At one of my latter celebrations in Ministry, a question was posed, "What has your *Yes!* cost you?" The woman of God, the word bearer, began to lay out the foundation, before the people with whom I had traveled. When I reflect back on this question, I am still moved by the substance and weight that it carries. In this brief but powerful synopsis of sharing my experiences, my *Yes!* cost me:

- Time
- Talent
- Timidity
- Temperance
- Total self-sacrifice
- Giving up
- Understanding the mandate
- Blood, sweat, tears
- Sleepless nights
- Fasting/praying

I was never alone. *If God be for us, who can be against us? (Roman 8:31)* God placed some supportive males (spiritual father, brothers) in my life to assist with my transformation. My interaction with male clergy has been positive. I was given instructions by way of the Holy Ghost, through my spiritual father,

"Another man cannot Lord over me." My covering is my husband and Jesus. I understand the importance of submission. *For lack of guidance a nation falls, but victory is won through many advisers (Proverbs 11:14).* My Yes! has allowed me to open doors for other apostles to come forth. I was blessed to develop a sisterhood, teaching how to empower the people of God. I have consecrated over 12 apostles and there is still much work to do.

The word of God is our daily reminder of how we operate in kingdom principles. My words of wisdom to the upcoming woman apostle are:

Refer to Scripture for support.

1. Make sure the Lord called you. *Peter 1:10*
2. Don't do it for vain glory. *I Corinthians 10:31*
3. Don't operate in pride. *Proverbs 16:18*
4. Stay focused and trust God for your every move. *Proverbs 3:5-6*
5. Fast/pray. *Matthew 17:21*
6. Let the word of God be your leader. *II Timothy 2:15*
7. Walk in integrity. *St. John 16:13*
8. If you don't know, get help. *James 1:5*
9. Don't suffer in silence. *Proverbs 11:14*
10. Find a John. *Proverbs 17:17*

We all have heard of prominent leaders who have decided for various reasons they just can't do it anymore. I was asked the question, "Apostle Wilson, why do you still do what you do?" Without hesitation, "I do it because there is always a soul waiting." I stand on Isaiah 54:1 and Luke 10:19. This book is being penned because we wanted to encourage the men to be an olive branch. We are better together than separated. I don't do it for glory because no one knows the story but God and me. Many can be charged with being an apostle, but it comes with work. As the Shunammite woman proclaimed, "It is well." Price was paid on Calvary. I don't do it because I have to, but I have a passion for the souls. If I can help somebody along the way, then my living is not in vain. The following books are recommended for everyone's personal library: The Bible (word of God), *Hinds Feet in High Places, Pilgrim's Progress, Pigs in a Parlor* and *Spiritual Authority.*

CHAPTER ELEVEN

JOURNEY OF A SERVANT

When we have our first real encounter with God, it is indescribable. From that moment, our lives are never the same. Real relationship with God invokes real hunger, according to Matthew 5:6: *Blessed are they which do hunger and thirst after righteousness: for they shall be filled.* As we were babes in Christ, we innocently say Yes! to God. At that point in our journey, there is such a seeking in our spirit; we never get tired of communing with the Father. We readily walk in submission and obedience unto God. Our Yes! permeates from within and soon we lose focus on how many times we said, Yes! It doesn't matter because that has become our lifestyle. Reflect back on being in His presence with your spirit in perfect alignment with His spirit. This feeling is priceless. It's a setup, but a blessing to be connected with our Creator, Yahweh God.

Relationship requires intimacy (into me you see). Even though God knows you, according to Jeremiah 29:11, He desires to be in covenant with all His children. It is during this time of communion, God begins to give us a glance at our future and the purpose concerning our lives. Revelation of our future can leave one speechless, but few even count up the cost. Be assured: Between purpose and promise, you must go through your process.

What happens when you discover that the anointing is not enough? *Christ* means the *Anointed One* or the *Chosen One. Christian,* its purest form, means *follower of Christ.* To be a "real Christian," means you have been anointed and chosen for purpose. We are to value what has been placed inside of us and never take the giver, God, for granted. On our journey from purpose to promise, God knew that we would need guidance, instruction, correction and discipline to prepare and support us. Omnipotent as God is, He strategically set up divine order to enhance the kingdom of God, according to Romans 13:1: *Let every soul be subject unto the higher powers. For there is no power but of God; the powers that be are ordained of God.* I remember a familiar saying, "Bloom where you are planted." First, are you planted in God's set place for your life? This is key, for you must receive the proper nutrients and watering to grow into the promise. Many miss this step, preferring to be included in what is popular at the time. Many mothers have explained to their children, while encouraging them by saying, "It may not be good to you, but it is good for you." Just as we don't get to choose our natural family, we don't choose our spiritual family either. We can attempt to attach ourselves to other houses, but a yielded vessel will find itself returning home.

Jesus said, in St. John 14:2-3, *I go to prepare a place for you. And if I go and prepare a place for you, I will come again and receive you unto myself; that where I am, there ye may be also.* What an awesome God we serve! He is very detailed about our heavenly position. He is that same detailed God who is mindful of where he has chosen to place each of us in the earthly realm. Unequivocally Yes! *And I will give you pastors according to my heart, which shall feed you with knowledge and understanding (Jeremiah 3:15).* God forever remains the God of order. In this life we don't always know what is good for us, but we must trust that our Heavenly Father does. Knowing this Proverbs 3:5-6 must become a part of your process. As we cross paths with our leader who has been chosen by God, there is almost instantly a connection. As Jesus walked, He simply told His disciples, "Follow me." I refer to this as the "honeymoon phase." You both are enjoying the newness of the relationship. The challenges don't really come until we begin the transformation phase.

And be not conformed to this world but be ye transformed by the renewing of your mind (Romans 12:2). Have you considered all the parties involved to assist you with this process, which includes you, God, and your leader who has been assigned to you?

We are easily drawn to the anointing; however few have real insight as to what it takes to walk with men and women of God. It can appear to be a life of excitement or glamour, but it's so much more. As a Believer, we find ourselves operating in certain positions in the body of Christ, and we must be able to identify if we are providing service, being a servant or being sold out.

- Service – The action of helping or doing work for someone
  As you see a need, you may or not decide to assist with what is needed (Refer to Romans 12:1).
- Servant – A person who performs duties for others
- Sold out – No limits or boundaries; total commitment

All three of these stages are needed in the body of Christ. As we mature in Christ, we should find ourselves growing in our commitment unto the Father. We start out by providing service but our desire should increase to the point where we want to be sold out telling God, I am all in. Many times we allow life events to stagnate our commitment unto God. Many know how to be a servant but we pick and choose when it is convenient. God is not a God of convenience, and He has given nothing but the best! To be sold out unto the kingdom of God is a choice. Will I serve you, Lord?

- In my affliction
- If I have to walk alone
- When it causes for sacrifice
- When I don't know the purpose *but I trust your plan*

This is the level of commitment that our leaders are walking in today and they need the people of God to operate in their kingdom positions so we can advance the kingdom of God. As a Believer, do you know the purpose as it relates to your life? Have you been given an assignment as it pertains to your leader? Are you providing a service or seeking a place of being sold out? If leaders received monetarily, for all the times they have been told, "The Lord told me that I am to walk with you in ministry," the church would have an overflow. We see them start out strong and then stop. Why? Some of the following reasons may be valid:

1. God didn't say it; you were zealous.
2. You didn't wait for instructions from God.
3. You moved out of the timing of God.
4. You were distracted by keeping your eyes

on the creature and not the Creator.
5. You couldn't get pass your past.
6. You didn't like walking alone.
7. The price was just too high.

There are many reasons why we may not complete the assignments we are given. Much consideration needs to be given that our leaders have walked the same paths that we are experiencing today. They also have sat in the seat of decision as to whether to obey God or not to obey. What if they would have made a different choice? How would that have affected your life? Remember: You were assigned to them. If they had not said, Yes!, will you be the person that you are today? Our church motto is very powerful, "Now we are the body of Christ Deliverance Ministries. One body, many members, working together for one common goal, that souls be saved and advance the kingdom of God. *Now* love somebody." God said, *If ye love me, keep my commandments (Refer to John 14:15-21).* As a servant, what we say must be in alignment with the heart of God in order to be effective in the kingdom of God. You may ask, what does this have to do with the apostolic woman? Even through elevation, you never stop being a servant. We must know how to be number 1 at being number 2, in order to be an effective leader of God. Until we know our leaders, through the heart of God, we will never comprehend the essence of who they are and our divine connection to them. *Can two walk together except they be agreed? (Amos 3:3)* It is our servant hood that will determine what type of leader we will become.

Again, I must reiterate that we are better together than separate. This book was intended to share with you the importance of the body of Christ working together to advance the kingdom of God. It is my prayer that hearts were transformed through the words that were written. We are all vital and necessary in the body. God has strategically placed us in the body because He alone knows our strengths through the Holy Ghost.

The battle that we face today is real, and it is going to take committed men and women of God to take a stand for righteousness. The only hindrance to the anointing of God is the unwillingness to submit to the Spirit of God.

The word of God refers to us as vessels and servants. As a vessel and servant we make ourselves available to be used in the kingdom. Men look at the outer appearance but God looks at the heart. We must find ourselves daily examining our hearts to make sure that it is perfect and upright before God. We are to find ourselves in a place of supporting, connecting with one another, building relationships, and seeking to empower others. The world is already trying to discredit our God. They use Biblical principles in their business to prosper but do not glorify the Lord. Men and Women of God: We are the salt of the earth (Refer to St. Matthew 5:13). Let us make sure that we are not losing our savor. Let us be very sure that our witness in the earth is not dimmed by our actions. We are in this world but not of this world. I admonish every Believer that is naming the name of Christ to walk worthy in the vocation by which ye are called. Learn to bloom where you are planted. Wherever God has called you, be faithful unto the assignment._Make sure you know the Lord has called you. Make sure that you are in the timing of God. Make sure that you have made full proof of your ministry.

Ministry is much greater than four walls of our various churches. True Ministry begins in our homes, our families, our communities and beyond…

It is my prayer that you have gained clarity of the apostolic woman. My pastor, Chief Apostle Dr. Yvonne Lee-Wilson, is the woman whose life has been chronicled in this work. I have travelled with Apostle Wilson and witnessed her laborious efforts to ensure the well-being of God's people and to speak truth to the lost soul through the teachings of Christ. It is amazing that we still do not know what "Yes" to the Father has cost her! I am grateful that God has trusted and graced us with a woman of God who truly loves His people and desires to advance His kingdom. This is not the end but the beginning of new chapters in her life. Keep reading…

CHAPTER TWELVE

THE VOICE THAT BEARS TRUTH

When I begin to reflect on this journey, I rejoice and give thanks to my Lord and Savior for saving my life! I can recall so vividly when I lie in the bed, wracked in pain, and the enemy wanted me to believe it was all over... Guess what? It was all over! I had fallen into the hands of God. He has called and chosen me for such a time as this... My present life is a gift, and I am careful of how to handle the work which the Lord has entrusted to me. He has ordained me to do preach the Gospel of Christ, before I was formed in my mother's womb. Therefore, I refuse to allow others to undermine the calling and grace of the Apostolic Woman.

The Mission to teach the Good News is marked by adversity and persecution. It is all part of God's plan, for the work which I have been called to employ in the Kingdom. Though I have been in a place, where the enemy could have silenced me, God allowed me to tell my story and speak truth through the teachings of Christ, so others may be healed, delivered, and set free! Many would say that I am a survivor. *I am more than a conqueror,* according to Romans 8:37.

As I begin to analyze the meaning of the *Voice* that

bears truth, I am reminded of the many voices that speak but are just uttering words. Intentions to glorify the Lord do not grace the center of one's purpose. They may have experienced pain but their hearts have been hardened. Their faith has been tested and they feel as though they have failed. Their self-righteous spirit has allowed them to justify actions that do not glorify God.

I am making reference to the voice that wants to be heard, solely to gain the attention and respect of others. I am speaking of the voice that seeks recognition, approval or public praise. I am discussing the motif of the voice whose aim is to deceive and undermine God's people. I am exposing the false prophet, workers of iniquity, imps.

The Apostolic Woman bears truth which travels on a wavelength, from the crest to the trough. It is the incorruptible Word that breaks down barriers, stereotypes, genders, and anything contrary to pleasing the Lord.

The Apostolic Woman makes her boast in the Lord, for she is constantly seeking His approval!

The Apostolic Woman educates, encourages, and empowers others to exercise self-accountability and responsibility, to connect with purpose, and *do all to the glory of God* (Refer to I Corinthians 10:31).

The Apostolic Woman edifies and uplifts others. She propels others to kingdom activity.

The Apostolic Woman upholds a lifestyle which aligns with precepts/principles of the Word.

The Apostolic Woman does not function in the vein of the world's role expectations of women but operates under the influence of the Holy Spirit.

The Apostolic Woman faces great adversity and persecution, for the Bible says, *Everyone who wants to live a godly life in Christ Jesus will be persecuted (2 Timothy 3:12).* The Apostolic Woman refuses to back down! Her confidence and faith are girded in the Promises of God! *If we suffer, we shall also reign with him: if we deny him, he also will deny us (2 Timothy 2:12).*

The Apostolic Woman is called and chosen by God. She makes her calling and election sure, to prevent from stumbling, for she adheres to 2 Peter 1:4-10. The Apostolic Woman exhibits knowledge of God's directives which are applied to every area of her life.

The Apostolic Woman is the *Voice* that Bears Truth, *The Only Truth which will remain forever and shall set you free! Refer to St. John 8:27-32.*

12 *DO'S & DON'TS*
OF THE APOSTOLIC WOMAN

The Apostolic Woman encourages us to:

1.   Study the word of God (II Timothy 2:15).

2.   Fast & pray often (Mark 9:29).

3.   Surround yourself with a strong support system (I Thessalonians 5:12).

4.   Find a *John,* according to the word, whom you can trust (Amos 3:3).

5.   Respect your mate, if you are married. If you are single, uphold respect for parents, so that you can function in every arena of daily living (Ephesians 5:22; Exodus 20:12).

6.   Keep a prophet close to you (Jeremiah 1:12).

7.   Have an intercessor in your life (James 5:16).

8.   Develop an apostolic team (Ephesians 4:11).

9.   Rest and replenish as often as needed (1 Corinthians 6:19).

10. Love without conditions and stand in the midst of any storm (I Peter 4:8; Ephesians 6:13).

11. Have a merry heart and enjoy Ministry (Proverbs 17:22).

12. Have a multitude of wise counsel (Proverbs 11:14).

The Apostolic Woman commands us to refrain from:

1.   Disrespecting authority *because* of your position (Romans 13:1)

2.   Trying to validate *who you are* or your calling (Romans 8:30)

3.   Stop being teachable (James 4:7).

4.   Allowing people to cause you to be prideful (Proverbs 16:18)

5.   Forgetting that you must have the Holy Spirit (John 16:13; John 14:26)

6. Lying to yourself, when challenged in your personal life (Hebrews 4:12)

7. Forgetting to walk by faith (2 Corinthians 5:7)

8. Forgetting you are not an island (1 Corinthians 12:27)

9. Forgetting to study and apply the word to your life daily (Psalm 119:105)

10. Forgetting to advance the kingdom of God to increase your territory (Acts 1:8)

11. Forgetting to respect your peers and the people who support you (John 13:35)

12. Losing your anointing by compromising (Proverbs 4:23)

EPILOGUE

BIRTHING OUT

It is my prayer that you have received insight not just about the Apostolic Woman but the body of Christ as a whole. Revelation with application is fruitless. We are to be fruit bearers according to St. John 15:2…and every branch that beareth fruit, he purgeth it, that it may bring forth more fruit. So, congregation of the righteous, my question to you is what are you birthing out? Where do we go from here? Are you using the power in your tongue correctly? We need to be sure that those things which bless God are nurtured, until the vision that God has concerning us comes to fruition. Other things that don't give God glory and is not in alignment with His will we need to speak so that it may dry up from the root.

The body of Christ is God's greatest investment and He continues to labor with us in love until we come into the unity of the faith. When you are connected to the body of Christ, it's no longer just about you. Therefore, your actions not only affect you, but it affects the entire body. Naturally, the body truly is unique and designed to heal itself. Our immune systems are fighting even when we don't know that we are experiencing a health crisis. All parts of the body are important. There is a spiritual application concerning the body as well. The body of Christ is designed to operate in oneness. When the oneness is compromised the body finds itself challenged.

We know that it is not about titles, but it is about being strategically positioned by God so that he can get the glory and the body of Christ be edified. If He called you, answer the call and know that you are qualified because of the spirit of God that dwelleth in you. Man looks at the outer appearance, but God looks at the heart. What God has ordained it can't be changed by a man. Isaiah 55:11 says, "So shall my word be that goeth forth out of my mouth; it shall not return unto me void, but it shall accomplish that which I please, and it shall prosper in the thing whereto I sent it." Know that God has the final say about you. The body of Christ is impregnated with God's word, purpose, promise and destiny. We cannot afford to have spiritual abortions, miscarriages, premature, and overdue deliveries in the body of Christ because souls are at stake.

- **Abortion** is a procedure that deliberately terminates a pregnancy. When we go against God's plan concerning our lives, we are deliberately telling God, I won't allow the assignment to be completed through me. Whosoever shall deny me before men, him will I also deny before my Father which is in heaven. (Matthew 10:33).

- **Miscarriage** is the expulsion of a fetus from the womb before it can survive independently. A seed was planted, and it was establishing roots, but no life came forth. And some fell among thorns and the thorns grew up and choked it and it yielded no fruit. (Mark 4:7)

- **Premature** is occurring or done before the usual or proper time; too early. You may have been given an assignment by God, but you went ahead of Him. When God gives assignments, we must wait for instructions. For my thoughts are not your thoughts, neither are your ways my ways, saith the Lord (Isaiah 55:8). Through zeal we run with the vision and it doesn't manifest in its totality. This does not mean that God didn't say it. We just need more direction.

- **Overdue Birth** is not having arrived, happened, or been done by the expected time. Many times, when we find that we are in a state of overdue it is usually because we have allowed something to hold us back. It could be afraid of the unfamiliar, lack of trust, inadequacy, etc. Whatever it is, this will have the same impact as being aborted. But without faith it is impossible to please him, for he that cometh to God must believe that he is, and that he is a rewarder of them that diligently seek him. (Hebrews 11:6).

When a woman has carried a pregnancy to full term, she travails to bring forth life; she utilizes every ounce of her strength to make sure that life comes. She doesn't think of what the bringing forth of life will cost her, but her focus is on the result and that is making sure she completes what she was designed to do.

It is my prayer that the reader of this book will allow the words to penetrate your spirit and allow God to use you as a vessel unto honor, meet for the master's use. Just like that mother who gave birth to her child, allow God to use you to bring life unto the body of Christ. Don't think about what you think it might cost you because my bible says that no man has left house, or brethren, or sisters, or father, or mother, or wife, or children, or lands, for my sake and the gospel's. But he shall receive a hundredfold now…and in the world to come eternal life. There is a song that says, "You can't beat God giving, no matter how hard you try." You want your purpose to be fulfilled in your life? How bad to you want it? Greatness is in you, but you must allow it to be birthed out. You need to know that it's going to cost you something. Your yes to God upsets the enemy but know that no weapon that is formed against you shall prosper.

Whether you have been called to the offices of the 5-Fold Ministry or wherever God has position you, this book was designed to provoke you and to thrust you out into the deep. Just as God is raising up Apostles in this season, He has also not only assigned but equipped both men and women to walk with them to advance the kingdom of God. To quote Apostle Heidi Ellis, "you must know your place, get in your place and stay in your place." Don't allow anything or anyone to move you from where God has positioned you. To those who are experiencing elevation, know that with elevation comes intense spiritual warfare. The way up is down on your knees in prayer and humbling yourself to stay at the feet of Jesus. And from the days of John the Baptist until now the kingdom of heaven suffereth violence, and the violent take it by force. We have much work to do. If you are reading this book, it is because it was ordained by God. Let us not just be hearers of the word but apply what you read. Know this, the body of Christ is not restricted within the four walls of a building. It lives in each of us who have made our calling an election sure and for all who are naming the name of Christ. Know your purpose, embrace you process and allow greatness to be birth out of you. Ye are of God, little children, and have overcome them; because greater is he that is in you, than he that is in the world. (1 John 4:4).

MINISTRIES OF SUPPORT

- Bishop Arthur M. Cofield (Spiritual Father in glory)
- Chief Apostle Dr. Joanna Bean (Spiritual Mother)
- Pastor Dr. Brenda Y. Smith – *Changed Lives Ministry*
- Pastor Patricia Kidd – *Power Prayer Partners Ministry for Prosperity*
- Pastor Constance Crawford – *I Prefer Jesus Ministries*
- Apostle Denise Clark – *House of Rhema Praise & Worship*
- Pastor Larry & Dr. Faye Rogers – *Israel Community Methodist Church*
- Apostle Robbie Peters – *House of Empowerment Church*
- Apostles Christopher & Heidi Ellis – *Fresh Anointing Ministries*
- Apostle Carol Sherman Ministries
- T.K. Sherman Ministries
- Dr. Harriet P. Jamison – *Harvesting for Souls*
- Apostle Joe Pitts – *Mission of Love Full Gospel Church*
- Pastor Rod Parsley – *World Harvest Church, Columbus Ohio*

- Pastor Olivia Paige – *God Sent Breakthrough*
- Pastor Octavia Morgan – *Sisters' Labor of Love*
- Prophet Beverly Holmes – *Visions of the Future*
- Chief Apostle Dr. Sylvester Brinson, III
- Pro-Life/Pro-Family Coalition
- Apostle Debra Gaines
- Apostle Dr. Elsie Bridges – Atlanta Georgia
- Apostle Dr. Shaunette Houghton – *Labors for Christ*
- Dr. Verndale Sheldon – *Living Sacrifices*
- Apostle Beverly London
- Pastor Napoleon & Evangelist Betty Hollister – *Greater King David Church*
- Apostle Virgil Jones
- Apostle Saundra Yancy
- Chief Apostle Katherine Miles
- Overseer Larry & Apostle Barbara Jefferson – *JOMP*
- Apostle Deborah Alexander

By the grace of God and the Holy Spirit that lives within me, I am the Apostolic Woman in this book! My heartfelt thanks go out to Bishop Dr. Arthur M. Cofield, my spiritual father and Evangelist Mother Shirley Cofield, in addition to Evangelist Rose Jones, Pastor

E.R. Allen, Bishop Clarence Lee, Apostle James Brown Jr., Apostle Patricia Fergerson, Minister Betty Donaldson, Pastor Gwen Bonds, and Apostle Dr. Richard D. Henton. These are generals who have gone to see the King and released their mantle upon me.

Praise God I have been One sent to advance the kingdom of God! We shall continue to stand in solidarity on our motto: "Now we are the body of Christ Deliverance Ministries, One body, many members, working together for one common goal-that is for souls to be saved and advance the kingdom of God (I Corinthian 12:27a).

To my brother, Bishop Dr. Anthony Lee, thank you for standing with us and giving us truth. Everyone needs a prophet, especially one who will not compromise and that is you, Prophet Dr. Taneshia Lee, my daughter. You always help me to see my "Why".

Although this story has been inspired by many, I want to acknowledge two amazing young women who helped me to birth this vision and bring it to pass – Evangelist Tonya Harris and Sister Kelly Gandy. Thank you for listening to the heart of an apostle and believing in the vision of The Apostolic Woman.

Last but never the least, Elder Louise Snipes, my mother, I love you for giving me the best gift ever, and that was Jesus.

 I have sent out and ordained many, but exemplary models for the Body of Christ Deliverance Ministries are: Pastor Dr. Brenda Yvonne Smith of *Changed*

Lives Ministries. Dr. Smith is a leader of leaders who understands true vision of the apostolic woman. The first apostle coming directly from Body of Christ Deliverance Ministries, June 29, 2018, is Dr. Barbara Jefferson and Overseer Larry Jefferson of *JOMP (Jesus Operates Miracles Profoundly).* Thank God for the anointing to serve within their lives.

What is a book without my *A-Team,* the ministerial staff of the Body of Christ Deliverance Ministries? I extend a sincere thank you to Pastor Rochelle Brantley, Pastor Olivia Paige, Pastor Octavia Morgan, Pastor Lolita Luckett, Evangelist Bessie Williams, Evangelist Tonya Harris, Minister Tracie Richardson, Minister Elaine Presberry, Minister Sheila Love, Minister Marie Parker and Minister Latonja Golden.

To my pastor, Dr. Brenda M. Brown, who has supported the vision for over 30 years and is still standing with us: Thank you! You are greatly appreciated!

To my Spiritual Mother Chief Apostle Joanna Bean, thank you for always believing and pouring inside of me the word that comes alive when you walk by faith and trust God. (Jeremiah 33:3).

Every apostle would be blessed to have an armor bearer. I give God glory for Evangelist Constance T. Crawford who is now a pastor of her own church, *I Prefer Jesus Ministries.* Thank you for your patience, time, talent, alms, fasting and praying, but most of all, walking by faith and not by sight to fulfill your assignment. This is not the end, but the beginning of more to come of the apostolic woman.

<u>Other Books by Apostle Dr. Yvonne Lee-Wilson:</u>

The Rise & Fall of Women in Ministry
The Rise & Fall of Women in Ministry: *The Journal*
365-Day Devotional Journal
for Intercessors and Prayer Warriors

Professional Life Coach/Consultant
P.O. BOX 288813
Chicago, Illinois 60628
Email: drywilson@gmail.com

www.ingramcontent.com/pod-product-compliance
Lightning Source LLC
Chambersburg PA
CBHW060546100426
42742CB00013B/2476